What the Bible *Really* Says about Homosexuality

*T*he law of the Lord is perfect, reviving the
soul;
the decrees of the Lord are sure, making
wise the simple;
the precepts of the Lord are right, rejoicing the heart;
the commandment of the Lord is clear, enlightening
the eyes;
the fear of the Lord is pure, enduring forever;
the ordinances of the Lord are true and righteous
altogether.
More to be desired are they than gold, even much fine
gold;
sweeter also than honey, and dripping of the honey-
comb.

Psalms 19:7-10

What the Bible
Really Says
about
Homosexuality

Daniel A. Helminiak, Ph.D.

foreword by
John S. Spong
Episcopal Bishop of Newark, NJ

ALAMO SQUARE PRESS
San Francisco, CA

Library of Congress Catalog Card Number: 94-070336

ISBN: 0-9624751-9-X

10   9   8   7   6   5   4   3   2

To lesbian women and gay men
who believe in a good God and reverence the Bible
and who also want to be able to believe in themselves

Table of Contents

*L*et us therefore no longer pass judgment on
one another,
but resolve instead never to put a stumbling
block or hindrance in the way of another.
I know and am pursuaded in the Lord Jesus that
nothing is unclean in itself;
but it is unclean for anyone who thinks it unclean.

Romans 14:13-14

Foreword

There is no book I love more nor one that has shaped my life more dramatically than the Bible. Yet, had I not escaped the literalism of my Christian fundamentalist upbringing, I could not make that statement, for long before now I would have either dismissed the Bible as a hopelessly ignorant and prejudiced ancient religious document or I would have denied reality and become myself a small-minded religious bigot, using literal scriptures to justify my prejudices. A literal Bible, in my opinion, admits no other options.

In my priestly and episcopal career I have watched the literal Bible be quoted to justify racial segregation, to ensure the continued sexist oppression of women by the Christian church, and to perpetuate a killing homophobia in our corporate life.

Had I lived in an earlier part of history, I would have seen the Bible quoted to condemn Copernicus, who asserted that the sun did not occupy the center of the universe, and Galileo, who said that the sun did not rotate around the earth. I would have seen the insights of Isaac Newton challenged by a biblical view of God that

9

could only be described as supernatural magic. I would have witnessed the church's attack upon Charles Darwin in the name of a brand of creationism that today is totally dismissed. Perhaps worst of all, I would have watched while religious people appealed to the literal text of the Bible to support the most inhumane treatment of fellow human beings—the institution of slavery.

In this volume, Daniel A. Helminiak, a Roman Catholic priest, brilliantly and courageously explores the biblical texts which are today used to condemn, oppress and marginalize God's children who are gay and lesbian. He brings to his scriptural analysis the heart of a Christian pastor who has stood beside the victims of a virulent prejudice. He goes beyond the literal words of the text to enter into the spirit of the Bible, where he confronts a God who created us all in the divine image, a Christ who values each of us infinitely and a Holy Spirit who calls us into the fullness of our humanity. He dares to set aside the culturally conditioned biblical words for the power of his Lord, who embraced the outcasts of his society whether they were lepers, Samaritans or those who were thought to be possessed by demonic spirits.

Father Helminiak's words will bring hope to many who feel that God has rejected them, and his book will help to make the church aware that it cannot claim to be the body of Christ if it fails to welcome all whom Christ would welcome. His work will also engender hostility, maybe even in official church circles. That is always the way it is when prejudices are challenged, even the prejudices of those who claim to speak for God.

I welcome his work and commend it to all who seek to know both the heart of Christ and the work of God that sometimes works unseen and unrecognized beneath the words of scripture.

The Right Reverend John S. Spong
Bishop, The Diocese of Newark
The Episcopal Church

Preface

Since 1977, in Boston, San Antonio and Austin, I have ministered as a Roman Catholic priest to the lesbian and gay community—mostly through Dignity. Dignity is a support group for lesbian, gay and bisexual Catholics and their friends.

I have come to know the gay community probably as well as anybody, and I have become aware of too many horrors:

- Thirty to 40 percent of the youth living on the streets are teenagers who were thrown out or left their homes because they are homosexual.
- Thirty percent of teenage suicides are among homosexual youth. Proportionately, this figure is at least two to three times higher than for other adolescents.
- People lose their jobs because their boss does not like "queers."
- Parents lose custody of their children or visitation rights for being lesbian or gay.

• Men and women are evicted from their apartments or their houses are burned—because somebody said they were gay.

• Gay men and lesbians are routinely beaten up—and murdered—for being homosexual.

• Public officials make abusive comments about the homosexual minority and easily get away with it.

• A judge hands down a blatantly prejudiced judgment against a gay man's murderers and then is easily re-elected.

• A presidential administration and much of the nation ignore an epidemic that in the USA was initially most prevalent among homosexual men.

• A gay man dies of AIDS in his home, locked away from every outsider, without any medical attention, because his family did not want others to know.

• Much human potential is squashed and wasted in people who live for years in secret self-hatred, taught to be afraid of their own hearts.

And there is more, so much more, that most people never know. The standard media are selective in the news they report. Prejudice, downright loathing for homosexuals, is condoned in our society. All this I have come to know too well over the years.

Living in the Bible Belt since 1981, I came to another sad realization: Bible religion plays a major role in allowing those horrors to happen. Quote the Bible, and all discussion suddenly comes to an end. Supposedly, the Bible condemns homosexuality, and some people take that to mean that the Bible justifies hatred and cruelty against gays and lesbians.

Of course, bigotry will have its day, and it will claim to have God on its side—against Jews, against Muslims, against Blacks, against women, against gays. Thus has it always been.

But more reasoned voices also emerge from within religion.

12

Recent research on the Bible shows that, at the very least, the same-sex acts that are the focus of biblical concern were not what we mean by "homosexuality" today. The Bible conceived of the matter very differently in a very different world. Even more, this research shows that the Bible is basically indifferent to homosexuality in itself. The Bible is concerned, as with heterosexuality, only when practices violate other moral requirements.

This information needs to be shared. Lesbian and gay people, condemned on the basis of Bible quotes, need to be able to respond intelligently, knowing they are not rejecting God's word. People raised in a strict Bible tradition, struggling with the literal text, need to be able, in good conscience, to find compassionate teaching on homosexuality in the Bible. People who choose to follow the "literal reading" of the Bible need to understand how others, in good faith, can insist the Bible does not condemn homosexuality.

So I present this little book. My commitment to the common good compels me. My goal is to make current information available to people who simply cannot plow through scholarly tomes. My hope is to help diffuse the power of unthinking religion and prejudice and to foster a world that is more compassionate, loving and just.

This book is a popular presentation. I have written as simply as I am able. I do not cite all the historical evidence nor repeat all the intricate discussions. Without completely ignoring the important differences of opinion, I present just one consistent position.

I have agonized over parts of this text. If the conclusion comes down squarely on one side of the question, that is because I honestly believe the evidence falls that way. To be sure, this is not a position that everyone will welcome. Those who can show reason to read the evidence differently must certainly draw another conclusion. But all must at least admit that this book reports some of the best scholarly opinion of our day.

As a Roman Catholic—and more importantly, a thinking person—I do not presume the Bible provides the last word on sexual ethics. In my mind, the matter is more complicated than that.

Historical, cultural, philosophical, psychological, sociological, medical, spiritual and personal factors all come to bear on the matter. Nonetheless, biblical teaching is an important basis for any Judeo-Christian belief. And every opinion, religious or otherwise, should rest on facts.

To me this seems to be fact: the Bible supplies no real basis for the condemnation of homosexuality.

Therefore, people must stop opposing homosexuality merely by quoting the Bible, because, taken on its own terms, the Bible simply does not support their case. If they have some other reason for their opposition, they ought to get clear what that reason is and state it up front.

That is the challenge I pose with this book—for those who oppose homosexuality. For those who are homosexual or who support those who are, I offer this book as some consolation: the Bible is not against them. For those who are somewhere in the middle, not knowing where to stand, I hope this book will help them make an informed judgment.

I am indebted to many people in the preparation of this work, especially to the scholars who have done the hard research behind this book. I give them few specific credits in the text itself. To keep things simple I use no footnotes or references. The list of sources at the end of this book provides the names and works of these scholars, and the annotations suggest their main arguments and the history of the scholarly discussion. Anyone interested in further detail will find ample resources there.

I rely most heavily on the work of John Boswell, Professor of History at Yale University, and L. William Countryman, Professor of New Testament at the Church Divinity School of the Pacific, Berkeley, California. They have argued most cogently for a reinterpretation of the Bible texts on "homosexuality." Boswell's meticulous study of biblical terms pushed the scholarship to a new level of clarity, and Countryman's analysis of purity issues in Romans transformed the discussion. Countryman's is the most recent lengthy study and has taken all the others into account. For the most part, this book merely reports the original historical research of Boswell and Countryman.

However, I depart from Boswell and Countryman in my treatment of 1 Corinthians 6:9 and 1 Timothy 1:10, and I rely more heavily on Robin Scroggs, Professor of New Testament at Union Theological Seminary, New York City; David F. Wright, Senior Lecturer in Ecclesiatical History and former Dean of the Faculty of Divinity at New College, The University of Edinburgh, Scotland; William L. Petersen, Associate Professor of Religious Studies at The Pennsylvania State University; and Victor P. Furnish, University Distinguished Professor of New Testament at Perkins School of Theology, Southern Methodist University. Debate revolves around an obscure Greek term, *arsenokoitai*, and the weight of historical evidence suggests this term does intend some kind of male same-sex acts.

I am also grateful to other colleagues and friends—especially to Bishop John S. Spong for his gracious and kind Foreword to this book, to Mike Bathum for collaboration on an early idea to provide illustrations for this book, to Steven Tomlinson for very helpful suggestions on a number of successive drafts, and to Ricardo Langoria, Scott Moore, and Paul Whitaker Paré for extensive and detailed criticism on an early draft. I thank Bert Herrman of Alamo Square Press for his willingness to publish this Bible study and for his meticulous attention to this book at every stage of the publishing process. For feedback, criticism, ideas, information, encouragement and motivation, I thank Mark Adcox, Cheryl Amendola, John Dennis Anderson, Kerry Baker, Richard Beauchesne, Sylvia Chavez, L. William Countryman, H. Thomas Cunningham, Paul Dauben, James R. DeMuth (R.I.P.), Michael H. Floyd, James Michael Flynn, Jesse Gomez, C. Edward Harris, Jan Heemrood, David Henton, Bruce Jarstfer, Toby Johnson, David Jones, Frank Leclerc (R.I.P.), Raymond Machesney, Richard N. Marshall, Donna Mayfield, Don McMahon, Christopher Menzel, Robert Nugent,

William L. Petersen, Paula Rieder, William C. Spong, John Tessaro, Elisa Velasquez and John Welch. Of course, I take full responsibility for what is finally written here.

One. Introduction

"The Bible condemns homosexuality. It says so in black and white."

That is what some people claim, and they impressively back up their case with quotes from the Bible. But others claim the matter is not as simple as that. These others also believe in the Bible, but they do not believe the Bible condemns lesbian and gay sex. Who is right? What is going on?

This book is to help you understand what's going on and decide who is right. For the past fifteen to twenty years, professional scripture scholars have been studying homosexuality in the Bible. Research is now at a point where we can make a brief and accurate summary that lay people can understand. Such a summary is what you are now reading.

The social sciences indicate that anywhere from two to four percent of the population is exclusively homosexual. That is, they experience romantic attraction only toward members of their own sex. Some further proportion of the population is predominantly homosexual. This is a significant number of people. In comparison, recall that the Jewish population in the United States is between two to three percent of the total.

Many of those who are homosexual have been raised to believe in the Bible, and they have been told that it condemns homosexuality. They are really in a bind. Their family and friends, who know they are good people, also feel caught in a bind. It looks as if homosexual people have to give up their religion or else—which seems impossible—give up their sexuality.

That is no small matter. In fact, scientific study of sexuality, along with psychology, has been underway for barely a century. But it is already clear that sexuality goes to the core of a person.

Sexuality means much more than physical arousal and orgasm. Attached to a person's sexuality is the capacity to feel affection, to delight in someone else, to get emotionally close to another person, to be passionately committed to him or her. Sexuality is at the core of that marvelous human experience, being in love—to be struck by the beauty of another and be drawn out of yourself, to become attached to another human being so powerfully that you easily begin measuring your life in terms of what's good for someone else as well as for yourself.

Sexuality is part and parcel of the human capacity for love. For we are not just intellectual beings, making calculated decisions to cherish somebody; we are emotional and physical, too. All this is what it means to be a human being, and all this comes into play when human love is on the scene.

To have to be afraid to feel sexual is to restrain that noblest of human possibilities, love. It is to short-circuit human spontaneity in a whole array of expressions—creativity, motivation, passion, commitment, heroic achievement. It is to be afraid of part of one's own deepest self.

This is not to say that sex acts are a necessary part of every human love. This is not to say that people cannot live without having sex. It is only to say that people who are afraid of their sexuality are constantly in hiding from their own selves. As a result, they are handicapped in all their dealings with other people and especially in their capacity to love deeply. All interior growth is stunted when people repress their affection, for heartfelt passion is really the engine of human achievement.

So, in a profound and important way, for people to have to choose between religion and sexuality is to have to choose between religion and themselves. As we are coming to understand the matter today, it is to have to choose between God and human wholeness.

That choice seems too hard, and it does not seem to make sense. Mounting scientific evidence shows it is nobody's doing that people are lesbian or gay. There is no reason to believe that homosexuality in itself is in any way unhealthy. And there is no credible evidence that sexual orientation can be changed nor convincing argument that it should be. The sociological, the psychological, the biological evidence, all more and more surely points in the same direction. The fact is that some people just happen to be homosexual.

Most people are straight but some are lesbian, gay or bisexual. Some people are tall, and some are small. Some are black or brown, others are yellow, red or white. Some are men, more are women. Most are right-handed, but some are left-handed. There is a wide range of individual differences among human beings. Sexual orientation seems to be one of those differences.

According to faith, it is God who creates us. Divine Providence forms us as we are. Our genes, our temperaments, our time and place in history, our talents, our gifts, our weaknesses—all are part of God's inscrutable and loving plan for us. So somehow God must be behind the fact that some people are homosexual. Then why should God's word in the Bible condemn homosexuality? There must be a mistake in the reasoning somewhere.

Could it be that *they* are the mistake? That something has gone wrong with lesbian and gay people? That they are inherently flawed? Some would believe so. But then God must be evil or be playing some cruel trick, but that cannot be. God does not make junk. So there must be another answer.

The mistake must be in how the Bible is being read. This is the argument presented here.

This book looks into the matter. The investigation begins with a discussion of methods of interpreting the Bible. That discussion is perhaps the most important part of this book, for how one reads the Bible is the heart of the matter. In perfectly good faith, two different people reading the same text can come up with two different meanings. Understand how different approaches to the Bible can lead to very different conclusions and you have an illuminating perspective on the debates about homosexuality in the Bible or about any other biblical topic.

Chapter Two explains those different ways of reading the Bible. Chapters Three through Seven consider each of the Bible texts that supposedly talk about homosexuality. Chapter Eight deals with other biblical arguments about homosexuality, such as the importance of the Bible's positive teaching about heterosexuality. Finally, Chapter Nine states the conclusion of this investigation.

Two. Interpreting the Bible

People differ passionately about what the Bible actually teaches. What's going on? Who is right?

Who is right? It depends on how one reads the Bible!

What's going on? Different ways of reading the Bible!

How one reads the Bible, the way one interprets the texts—this is the key issue. The question is not, "What are the Bible texts on homosexuality?" Anyone could list and quote them. The question is, "How do you interpret these texts?" "How do you determine what these texts really mean?"

Some will say we should take the Bible as it reads and not "interpret" it. But "interpretation" simply means getting the meaning out of a text. In this sense, there is no reading the Bible or anything else without interpreting. Without a reader, a text is only words—markings on a page. In themselves these markings mean nothing. To have meaning, they have to pass through someone's mind. Understanding the words, determining the meaning of the text, is interpretation. Any time people read anything, they are interpreting.

Words Don't Always Mean What They Say

It is important to pay attention to the different ways of reading a text, especially when dealing with ancient texts, like the Bible. The words might suggest one thing to us in the Twentieth Century but have meant something very different to the people who wrote them long ago.

Take an example from everyday life. In the United States we have an expression: to be out in left field. To understand this expression you have to know something about baseball. Areas of the baseball field are called center, right and left field, as viewed from the batter's position. Most batters are right-handed. They swing from right to left. So they tend to hit the ball more often and more deeply into left field. When they do hit a ball into right field, the ball is not likely to go as far. So the player covering left field needs to be positioned far back in the field, far from the other players. In many ways the left fielder is isolated and out of touch, off in his or her own world. So to say someone is "out in left field" means he or she is disoriented, out of contact with reality, wrong, unconventional, loony.

Now, what if you spoke perfectly good English but knew nothing of baseball or American usage and you heard that expression for the first time? "You're wondering about Robert? He's out in left field." You might go out looking for Robert in a field somewhere off to the left! You understood the words, but you missed the point.

Of course, you could argue that the words mean what they say. You heard them, and you did understand them. They locate Robert in a field that is "left," and "left" is a direction opposite "right." After all, you do speak English! You could insist if you wanted, but everybody else would think *you're* out in left field.

Baseball was really the big thing in the '40s and '50s. Other concerns have since shared the scene. So to make the same point in the '60s and '70s, you might have said, "You're a real space cadet." Today you might say, "You just don't compute."

Those sayings have nothing to do with real fields, space travel or computers, and they all make the same point. But ignore the culture in which they belong and you'll miss the point despite understanding the words.

Jesus' Teaching about Simplicity

Take an example from the Bible. In three of the Gospels— Matthew 19:24, Mark 10:25 and Luke 18:25—Jesus says, "It is easier for a camel to pass through the eye of a needle than for a rich person to enter the kingdom of God." It sounds as if nobody who had lots of money could ever get into heaven, for certainly no camel could ever get through a needle's eye. At least that's what this saying suggests to us.

But in Jerusalem there was a very low and narrow gate through the city wall. When a caravan entered through that gate, the camels had to be unloaded, led through the gate crouching down, and then reloaded inside the city wall. That gate was called "the eye of the needle."

So what was Jesus saying? Understand something about his everyday world, and his meaning is obvious. Jesus was simply saying that it would be hard for the rich to get to heaven. They might first have to unload their material concerns. Jesus was again preaching his Sermon-on-the-Mount message about simplicity of life and single-heartedness.

What if similar considerations apply to the Bible texts on homosexuality? Maybe those texts do not mean what we have been taking them to mean.

Alternative Interpretations

Of course, the Gospels recount that the disciples objected to Jesus' teaching about the eye of the needle. "Then who could be saved?" they protested. And Jesus responded that nothing is impossible with God.

So you could take Jesus' teaching to apply to a real physical impossibility, to a real camel passing through the eye of a real needle. You could insist that God could work a miracle, if God wanted to. You could insist that this text is actually about trusting God to do what seems impossible. And your interpretation would, indeed, fit the text.

But now we have two very different interpretations. And we have two very different pictures—not only of the text in question but also different pictures of God, of Jesus and of religious faith.

One interpretation appeals to miracles. It portrays a God who intervenes to suspend the laws of the universe, and it sees Jesus as teaching faith in such a God. This interpretation presents a picture of people entering heaven because God stepped in to work a miracle in their lives. The other interpretation appeals to Divine Providence. It portrays a God who works through the ordinary functioning of the universe, and it sees Jesus calling us to live responsibly in this world. This other interpretation presents a picture of people entering heaven because they unloaded the false concerns that burden their lives.

Both pictures do allow that God is guiding our lives and our world. But when it comes to the crunch, the one expects a miracle from God, and it awaits a vision or a revelation to settle a question. The other approach, more down-to-earth, presumes that God is already and always working through things as they are and it is up to us to make the best of the circumstances God has allowed. The down-to-earth approach is not irreligious. It is brimming with trust in God. It embraces the world as God made it. It uses the intelligence God gave us. It resolves questions by honest appeal to the evidence. It makes decisions in loving concern for what is right and good. In sum, it accepts our God-given stewardship over the world and over our lives.

Is one approach better than the other? Well, the core Judeo-Christian beliefs support the down-to-earth approach. God created our world and saw that it was good. God's Son came down to earth and lived among us. Jesus did not expect God to save him from death, and God did not. Evidently, according to biblical teaching and apart from human misuse, the world that God created and redeemed is good enough for God. Should it not also be good enough for us? Should we not also be down-to-earth in our faith?

Of course, the Bible does portray God as working miracles. And to pray for a miracle is not wrong—unless there is no need for one. But when there is no need, Jesus' words to Satan apply to us: "Do not put the Lord your God to the test" (Matthew 4:7; Luke 4:12). Besides, if we actually believed that God is working in our lives regardless of how things go, would we ever really feel the need to pray for a miracle?

Might we not be testing God by reading a miraculous interpretation into the text about the eye of the needle? A perfectly reasonable alternative interpretation is available. To insist, nonetheless, on a miraculous interpretation—isn't this acting on whim? Isn't this expecting God to do extraordinary things simply because we would prefer it so?

The Literal Reading and the Historical-Critical Reading

This book will focus on two different approaches to interpreting the Bible: the "literal reading" and the "historical-critical" reading. These two are parallels to the miraculous and the down-to-earth approaches to religion.

The literal reading claims to take the text simply for what it says. This is the approach of Fundamentalism. It claims not to be interpreting the text but merely to be reading it as it stands. Clearly, however, even Fundamentalism follows a rule of interpretation, a simple and easy rule. The rule is that a text means whatever it means to somebody reading it today.

Compare the other approach, the historical-critical reading. The rule here is that a text means whatever it meant to the people who wrote it long ago. To say what a biblical text teaches us today, you first have to understand the text in its original situation and then apply the meaning to the present situation. Jesus' teaching about the eye of the needle, in the down-to-earth approach, is a good example.

Although on TV and radio we generally hear only the fundamentalist approach, all the mainline Christian churches support the historical-critical method. So the argument being presented here is not novel; on the contrary, it is absolutely standard with almost two centuries of study behind it. In fact, it was on the scene before Fundamentalism, which arose partially in opposition to it.

Of course, some of the churches back off from the historical-critical method when it comes to the Bible texts on homosexuality and some other questions—like divorce, the place of women in society and church, Jesus' understanding of himself, the organization of the early church, or the origin of Christian rituals like Baptism and Eucharist. The churches are wary of the conclusions that their own approved method of interpretation suggests.

Historical-critical study of the Bible oftentimes reverses some long-standing interpretations and raises very serious questions about religion and society. No wonder the churches are hesitant. They are sometimes left wondering what to teach. No wonder Fundamentalism has taken a harder line. The new historical input can leave the older understanding of religion dissolving before our eyes. It is important to appreciate the delicateness of this matter of biblical interpretation.

But it is also important not to hide from the facts as we now know them. To do so would be to violate a core value of the Judeo-Christian tradition. To do so would be to ignore a value for which Jesus lived and died—even as John 8:32 has Jesus say, "The truth will set you free."

This approach is called "historical" because it requires that you put the text back into its original historical and cultural context before you decide what it means. This approach is called "critical" because it requires careful thought and detailed analysis of the Bible. The word "critical" is not used here in the more familiar sense of "trying to find fault with something."

Inspiration and Inerrancy of the Bible

These two ways of reading the Bible are very different, but both agree that the Bible is God's word. Both agree that God inspired the Bible and that the Bible is "inerrant" or without error. So no one can dismiss the historical-critical approach by claiming that it does not respect the Bible as God's word. Of course, those two approaches explain inspiration and inerrancy differently.

Inspiration means that God moved the human authors to write what they wrote, so the Bible is God's word to us. The literal approach relies on miracles, so for it inspiration means that God's power overwhelmed the human authors. The words just flowed from them. Sometimes the human authors did not even understand what they were writing. Now we, centuries later, can recognize in the Bible a secret message that God miraculously hid there for our generation alone.

The historical-critical approach understands biblical inspiration differently. This approach will agree that what the human authors wrote may well have further meaning of which they themselves were not aware. But for the historical-critical approach, the mentality is down-to-earth. People often say things that mean more than they know, especially when they speak eternal truths of the heart—like "A thing of beauty is a joy forever" or "I will love you as long as I live" or "Trust in God, and all will be well." So as history unfolds, the Bible texts will naturally suggest new and deeper meanings. The most obvious example is how the early Christians saw references to Jesus in the Hebrew Scriptures.

Moreover, according to the historical-critical approach, the biblical writers were not entranced secretaries, taking dictation like robots or channelling messages as in a seance. Rather, the biblical authors were well aware of what they were writing. They were intelligent, free, creative, culture-bound human beings. And God respected all that. God used all that, their humanity and their culture, to express divine wisdom in a particular human form. Thus, what they wrote is not only their word but also the word of God. Accordingly, if you wanted to understand what God intended to say, the first step would be to understand what those human authors intended to say. For precisely that is what God inspired.

Granted that the Bible is the word of God, the Bible must be free from error. Thus, the question of biblical inerrancy enters the discussion. Again, the literal and the historical-critical approaches both accept inerrancy, but they understand it differently.

The literal approach would take words to mean exactly what they say. Hearing that Robert is a real space cadet, this approach would assume that he is truly a NASA astronaut. Similarly, reading in the first chapter of Genesis that God created the world in seven days, the literal approach would insist that the universe was formed in one week. For if creation did not happen that way, the Bible is mistaken.

In contrast, the historical-critical approach first asks, What is the point of the Genesis story of creation? What was the author intending to say? Well, the Bible intended to give a religion lesson, not a science lesson. The seven-day story of creation is just a way of making the point: God created the universe with wisdom, care and order. If science determines that the universe actually evolved over millions and millions of years, there is no conflict with the Bible. Through science we are simply coming to understand how God chose to create the world. Science helps us to grasp some bit of the order and wisdom that God built into the universe. But the fact that God created the universe remains as true as ever. There is no error in that teaching of Genesis.

Both the literal approach and the historical-critical approach hold that the Bible is God's word, inspired and inerrant. There is no disagreement here. But these two approaches do disagree on what is exactly God's word in the Bible. For God's "word" is not the markings on the page nor even the string of words in the sentences. Rather, God's word is the *meaning* of the words and sentences formed by the markings on the page. Disagreeing on how to determine what the Bible means, the two approaches disagree on what God's inspired and inerrant word is. They disagree about what the Bible teaches because they interpret the Bible differently.

Pluses and Minuses of the Literal Approach

These two approaches to interpreting the Bible have their advantages and disadvantages. Consider first the literal approach. It is easy. It has no elaborate guidelines. It appeals to common sense and requires no detailed study. All this is clearly an advantage—at least in the short run—because it makes religion simple.

But the literal reading also has disadvantages. Since this approach has no elaborate guidelines, different people can arrive at different meanings for any text they consider. All can claim that the text means what it means to them.

Then how do you settle the differences of opinion? In the end, the text will be taken to mean what any group of people come to agree on. Popularity decides what the Bible means. An influential preacher could even impose a personal view on a whole congregation.

But because many people believe something, doesn't necessarily make it right. The long history of slavery is a clear case in point. So the serious disadvantage here is that people may well end up believing not what God requires but simply what makes them comfortable and secure.

Another disadvantage is selective use of the Bible. That is, this approach tends to emphasize one text and overlook another. Preachers condemn lesbians and gays because the Bible mentions same-sex acts in passing. But the same preachers do not advocate slavery even though the whole epistle to Philemon and many other long passages support it (Ephesians 6:5-9; Colossians 3:22-4:1; 1 Timothy 6:1-2; 1 Peter 2:18). They do not encourage people to gouge out their eyes or cut off their hands even though Jesus' literal words suggest that remedy for temptation (Matthew 5:22-29). Those preachers often allow divorce even though Jesus' teaching taken literally condemns it (Matthew 5:32; Mark 10:1-12; Luke 16:18). They allow women to teach in Sunday school or to speak in church even though 1 Timothy 2:11-14 clearly forbids that. They allow women to come to church in expensive clothes or gold jewelry or pearls or to come to church without hats even though long passages oppose such things (1 Timothy 2:9-10; 1 Corinthians 11:1-16). The literal approach is almost forced to pick and choose as it applies the Bible. Otherwise some very unacceptable situations would arise.

Finally, the literal approach is hard pressed to address new issues—nuclear energy, surrogate motherhood, environmental pollution, the use of outer space, genetic engineering, organ transplants. The Bible never imagined these things, so it never really addressed them.

Of course, some will insist that God did speak of these things in hidden and symbolic ways. Some will claim that certain obscure Bible texts were really speaking about twentieth-century issues. But if this is so, in some cases a symbolic interpretation is allowed, and the rule of literal interpretation is abandoned. Then what is the rule for knowing when to interpret literally and when to interpret symbolically? Without changing rules in the middle of the game, the literal approach cannot use the Bible to answer pressing questions of our day.

Pluses and Minuses of the Historical-Critical Approach

The historical-critical method also has its advantages and its disadvantages. On the positive side, this approach can determine the meaning of a text objectively, following clear guidelines. All who accept this method can agree on the interpretation.

Because of this approach, there are now no important differences between Catholic and Protestant Bible scholars. All are in general agreement about the meaning of Bible texts. When differences do occur, they do not depend on one's Protestant or Catholic affiliation. The differences depend on the historical evidence scholars cite and on the arguments they propose.

The line that divides the Christian churches no longer falls between Catholics and Protestants. The line of division falls between those who follow a fundamentalist reading of the Bible and those who follow an historical-critical reading, and this line often cuts right through the middle of a single church or denomination.

That God really is working in human history, not somehow floating above it, is a core aspect of Judeo-Christian faith. So another advantage of the historical-critical method is that it takes history and God's working in history seriously. As history progresses, God guides the process and things really do change. There is development and novelty. According to this understanding, religion is not locked into its first-century form.

However, the historical-critical method has a serious disadvantage. It is not easy. It requires long and difficult study. Only specialists can apply it. This method makes Bible interpretation a technical science. Archeology, history, ancient languages, anthropology, minute analysis of words and texts are all required for proper interpretation.

And some texts will be left forever unexplained. If all memory of baseball were suddenly lost, no one might ever understand what being "out in left field" means. Likewise, if the historical information around some Bible text is lacking, we may never be able to determine what the text meant to say. The discussion about two texts in Chapter Seven, 1 Corinthians 6:9 and 1 Timothy 1:10, offers a good example. Historical argument can become very tenuous— simply because we may not have the historical information to deter-

31

mine what a crucial word or phrase was supposed to mean.

Moreover, according to the historical-critical method, the times really do change. We cannot expect to find simple answers to contemporary questions just by reading the Bible. To understand God's will for us, we have to apply the lessons of the past to the problems of today. So, besides knowing what the Bible meant, we have to study the current problem. Sensitive to God's Spirit, we have to rely on our own minds and hearts to decide what the Bible requires in the situations we now face. To do that, we have to be good people—open, honest and loving or, in a word, authentic. All this is very demanding.

Finally, it is possible that this method of reading the Bible may overturn long-accepted interpretations. It may turn out that some Bible texts do not mean what we took them to mean for centuries. Then difficult debate about sensitive social issues arises. Homosexuality is an obvious case in point.

What about Homosexuality in the Bible?

This book summarizes recent Bible research on homosexuality following the historical-critical method. Based on our understanding of historical-critical method, what conclusion about homosexuality should we expect? Consider the facts.

The scientific study of sexuality is barely a century old. We now know that homosexuality is a core aspect of the personality, probably fixed by early childhood, biologically based, and affecting a significant proportion of the population in virtually every known culture. There is no convincing evidence that sexual orientation can be changed, and there is no evidence whatsoever that homosexuality is in any way pathological. Since the Second World War a worldwide gay community has been forming and gaining a voice. Within that community, and especially among gay and lesbian religious people, loving, adult homosexual relationships have become a major concern.

All those developments are recent. Some of them are absolutely new to human history. They are part of a situation that the biblical authors never imagined, so it is not to be expected that the Bible expresses an opinion about them. What is to be expected is this: When the Bible does talk about same-sex behavior, it refers to it as it was understood in those ancient times. The biblical teachings will apply today only insofar as the ancient understanding of same-sex behavior is still valid.

Specifically, in biblical times there was no elaborated understanding of *homosexuality* as a sexual orientation. There was only a general awareness of same-sex contacts or same-sex acts, what can be called *homogenitality* and *homogenital* acts. Our question today is about people and their relationships, not simply about sex acts. Our question is about homosexuality, not mere homogenitality. Our question is about spontaneous affection for people of the same sex and about the ethical possibility of expressing that affection in loving, sexual relationships. Because this was not a question in the minds of the biblical authors, we cannot expect the Bible to give an answer.

Why must that be so? If the Bible condemned a particular act for whatever reason, shouldn't that act still be avoided without any further discussion? If God's word says it is wrong, isn't it wrong, period?

A thing is wrong for a reason. If the reason no longer holds and no other reason is given, how can a thing still be judged wrong? Simply that "God said it is wrong" is not a good enough answer, for the point remains even in the case of God: God also says things are wrong for reasons. That is to say, there is good sense, there is wisdom, in the morality that God requires. If there is not, then all morality is arbitrary, and God makes things right or wrong on divine whim. Then all thought about ethics should stop, for there would simply be no rationale to morality; there would be no reasonableness in what God requires. But such a conclusion is absurd. It is absolutely ridiculous. So there must be a reason why something is wrong, and it must be for that very reason that God forbids the thing.

Well, couldn't God have reasons that we cannot understand? Of course. But if that is the case, we could never know God's will—unless God revealed it to us. And where would God reveal it? One obvious answer is, "In the Bible, of course!"

That answer is perfectly valid. But it brings us right back to our starting point: How do we determine what God meant to say in the Bible? The options are still the same: the literal approach or the historical-critical approach.

This book deliberately follows the historical-critical approach to the Bible. The expectation is that God says something is wrong for a reason. The Creator built that reason into the structure of the universe. Human intelligence would be able to discern that reason. Accordingly, when there is no new reason for a thing's being wrong and a former reason no longer applies, there is no basis for saying the thing is wrong. The reason—*God's own reason!* —is simply not there.

Does God's word in the Bible condemn what we know today as homosexuality? Consider all the biblical passages that refer to this topic. Understand them in their original historical context. Evaluate the evidence with an open and honest mind. The text-by-text analysis that follows will help you draw your own conclusion.

Three. The Sin of Sodom: Inhospitality

The story of Sodom is probably the most famous Bible passage that deals with homosexuality—or, at least, is said to deal with it. This story is found in the book of Genesis, chapter 19, verses 1 to 11:

> The two angels came to Sodom in the evening; and Lot was sitting in the gateway of Sodom. When Lot saw them, he rose to meet them, and bowed down with his face to the ground. He said, "Please, my lords, turn aside to your servant's house and spend the night, and wash your feet; then you can rise early and go on your way." They said, "No; we will spend the night in the square." But he urged them strongly; so they turned aside to him and entered his house; and he made them a feast, and baked unleavened bread, and they ate. But before they lay down, the men of the city, the men of Sodom, both young and old, all the people to the last man, surrounded the house; and they called to Lot, "Where are the men who came to you tonight?

Bring them out to us, so that we may know them." Lot went out of the door to the men, shut the door after him, and said, "I beg you, my brothers, do not act so wickedly. Look, I have two daughters who have not known a man; let me bring them out to you, and do to them as you please; only do nothing to these men, for they have come under the shelter of my roof." But they replied, "Stand back!" And they said, "This fellow came here as an alien [Lot was not originally from Sodom], and he would play the judge! Now we will deal worse with you than with them." Then they pressed hard against the man Lot, and came near the door to break it down. But the men inside reached out their hands and brought Lot into the house with them, and shut the door. And they struck with blindness the men who were at the door of the house, both small and great, so that they were unable to find the door.

The visiting angels then warned Lot that God was going to destroy Sodom in a downpour of fire and brimstone. So Lot and his family escaped the town. However, Lot's wife disobeyed the command not to look back, and she was turned into a pillar of salt. Sodom and neighboring Gomorrah were destroyed, "and lo, the smoke of the land went up like the smoke of a furnace" (19:28).

A Common Interpretation of the Story

Since about the Twelfth Century, this story has been taken to condemn homosexuality. The very word "sodomite" was taken to refer to someone who engages in anal sex, and the sin of Sodom was taken to be male homogenital acts. So supposedly God condemned and punished the citizens of Sodom, the Sodomites, for homogenital activity.

What Does "To Know" Mean?

Indeed, there is a clear sexual reference in the story. Lot offers his daughters as sex objects to the men crowding around his door. His daughters were virgins. Lot said they did not know a man.

In the Bible, "to know" sometimes means "to have sex with." That is the meaning of the word in the Christian Testament (also known as the "New Testament") where the angel told Mary that she was to be the mother of Jesus. Mary wondered, "How can this happen, since I do not *know* man" (Luke 1:34)? The verb "to know" occurs some 943 times in the Hebrew Testament (also known as the "Old Testament"). In ten of those cases the word has a sexual meaning. The present text is one of those ten.

It is shocking to think that Lot would have offered his daughters to the Sodomites. This is a good example of how different Lot's culture was from our own. In that time the father of the house actually owned the women. They were his property. He was free do with them almost whatever he wanted. It would have been very costly for Lot to give his daughters to those men, financially costly. For no one would then want to marry those women, already "used." It is surprising that Lot preferred to let the men of the town rape his daughters than to let them abuse his houseguests.

What did the men of Sodom want with Lot's two visitors? They say they wanted "to know them." Some take this to mean the men wanted to have sex with the visitors. Lot's offering his daughters for sex in place of the male visitors certainly indicates as much. Still, others argue the word "to know" need not refer to sex. It may simply be that the men of Sodom wanted to find out who these strangers were and what they were doing in their town. After all, Lot was not a native of Sodom. He, too, was an outsider. The townsfolk were not happy with his inviting strangers in.

In the end there is no way of being absolutely certain whether this text refers to homogenital acts or not. In fact, most experts believe that it does. What is certain is that this text is concerned about abuse, not simply about sex.

As we will see below, in the many biblical references to the sin of Sodom, there is no concern whatever about homogenitality, but there is concern about hardheartedness and abuse. Allowing that the word "to know" really does have a sexual meaning here, what is at stake is male-male rape, not simply male-male sex.

The Duty of Hospitality

Why would Lot have been willing to expose his daughters to rape? Why would Lot object to the townsfolk interrogating and abusing the visitors? Lot was a just man or, as the Scriptures say, a righteous man. He did what was right, as best he could. Of all the people in Sodom, only he had the kindness to invite the travelers in for the night.

In desert country, where Sodom lay, to stay outside exposed to the cold of the night could be fatal. So a cardinal rule of Lot's society was to offer hospitality to travelers. The same rule is a traditional part of Semitic and Arabic cultures. This rule was so strict that no one might harm even an enemy who had been offered shelter for the night. So doing what was right, following God's law as he understood it, Lot refused to expose his guests to the abuse of the men of Sodom. To do so would have violated the law of sacred hospitality.

The Meaning of Male Anal Sex

If, in addition, the Sodomites did want sex with the town visitors, the offense against them would have been multiplied. For forcing sex on men was a way of humiliating them. During war, for example, besides raping the women and slaughtering the children, the victors would often also "sodomize" the defeated soldiers. The idea was to insult the men by treating them like women. So part and parcel of the practice of male-male anal sex was the notion that men should be "macho" and that women are inferior, pieces of property at the service of men.

In fact, throughout Western history, a main reason for opposition to male-male sex was that it supposedly makes a man act like a woman. Saint John Chrysostom in the Fifth Century and Peter Cantor in the Twelfth, outspoken Christian opponents of homogenitality, both raised that argument. To be the active partner was generally more acceptable, but to be the receptive partner was "unmanly." Evidently, the objection was more to a man's being "effeminate" than to his having sex with another man.

The Sin of Sodom

So what was the sin of Sodom? Abuse and offense against strangers. Insult to the traveler. Inhospitality to the needy. That is the point of the story understood in its own historical context.

When male-male rape becomes part of the story, the additional offense is sexual abuse—gross insult and humiliation in Lot's time and in our own. The whole story and its culture make clear that the author was not concerned about sex in itself. Lot offered his daughters without a second thought. The point of the story is not sexual ethics. The story of Sodom is no more about sex than it is about pounding on someone's front door. The point of the story is abuse and assault, in whatever form they take. To use this text to condemn homosexuality is to misuse this text.

The Bible's Own Understanding of the Sin of Sodom

That is the conclusion that follows from an historical-critical reading of the Sodom story. But in this particular case the meaning of the text is obvious from other parts of the Bible. For the Bible often refers back to the story of Sodom and says outright what Sodom's sin was.

The prophet Ezekiel (16:48-49) states the case baldly: "This was the guilt of your sister Sodom: she and her daughters had pride, surfeit of food and prosperous ease, but did not aid the poor and needy." The sin of the Sodomites was that they refused to take in the needy travelers.

According to Wisdom 19:13, the sin of Sodom was a "bitter hatred of strangers" and "making slaves of guests who were benefactors." Recall that the strangers, the guests, were actually angels on mission from God. The sin was to treat them abusively. The reference to "making slaves of guests" may refer to a common practice of the day wherein the master of a house would freely use the slaves for sexual purposes. But again, the offense was not in having sex nor even in keeping slaves but in taking advantage of, demeaning and abusing others.

Even Jesus makes reference to Sodom, and the issue is rejection of God's messengers:

> These twelve Jesus sent out with the following instructions: ". . . Whatever town or village you enter, find out who in it is worthy, and stay there until you leave. . . . If any one will not welcome you or listen to your words, shake off the dust from your feet as you leave that house or town. Truly I tell you, it will be more tolerable for the land of Sodom and Gomorrah on the day of judgment than for that town." (Matthew 10:5-15)

What is the reference in this gospel incident? There is no reference to sex. But there is a clear reference to rejection of God's messengers. The parallel between the gospel and Sodom is the closed heart that rejects the stranger, the wickedness that will not welcome God's heralds.

There are other less direct biblical references to Sodom: Isaiah 1:10-17 and 3:9, Jeremiah 23:14 and Zephaniah 2:8-11. The sins listed in those places are injustice, oppression, partiality, adultery, lies and encouraging evildoers.

Adultery is the only sexual sin in that list, and even in this case sex itself is not the concern. In the mind of the Hebrew Testament, adultery is not an offense against a woman nor against the intimacy of marriage nor against the inherent requirements of sex. Adultery is an offense against justice. Adultery offends the man to whom the women belongs. Adultery is the misuse of another man's property.

The Bible often uses Sodom as an example of the worst sinfulness, but the concern is never simply sexual acts. Least of all is the concern homogenital acts.

The Sin of Sodom Today

Even Jesus understood the sin of Sodom as the sin of inhospitality. Other passages in the Bible come right out and say the same thing. Yet people continue to cite the story of Sodom to condemn gay and lesbian people.

There is a sad irony about the story of Sodom when understood in its own historical setting. People oppose and abuse homosexual men and women for being different, odd, strange or, as they say, "queer." Lesbian women and gay men are just not allowed to fit in; they are made to be outsiders, foreigners in our society. They are disowned by their families, separated from their children, fired from their jobs, evicted from apartments and neighborhoods, insulted by public figures, beaten and killed on the streets. All this is done in the name of religion and supposed Judeo-Christian morality.

Such oppression is the very sin of which the people of Sodom were guilty. Such behavior is what the Bible truly condemns over and over again. So those who oppress homosexuals because of the supposed "sin of Sodom" may themselves be the real "sodomites," as the Bible understands it.

41

Four. The Abomination of Leviticus: Uncleanness

The specific concern in the story of Sodom is not homogenital acts. But there is one reference in the Hebrew Testament where that is the concern. Leviticus 18:22 states, "You shall not lie with a male as with a woman; it is an abomination." Then Leviticus 20:13, completing this reference, adds the punishment: "If a man lies with a male as with a woman, both of them have committed an abomination; they shall be put to death, their blood is upon them."

In this passage the Bible uses a roundabout way of talking: to lie with a male as with a women. The Hebrew text, translated literally, is even more obscure. It reads, "With a male you shall not lie the lyings of a woman." Nonetheless, there is no doubt that the text refers to male homogenital acts. There is no hint of lesbian sex acts here. The offense is called an abomination, and the prescribed penalty is death. This all sounds pretty straightforward, and it sounds pretty bad. But what does this text mean in its own historical context?

They Shall be Put to Death

First, consider the death penalty. It really is severe. But Leviticus prescribes the same penalty for cursing one's parents. Other sexual sins also merit the death penalty: adultery, incest and bestiality. The law in Leviticus considered all these crimes to be very serious—but for different reasons.

Cursing one's parents, for example, was a major crime against society. Israelite society of the time was built around the extended family, the clan or the tribe. Slaves were subject to the children of the household. The children in turn were subject to their parents, and the mother was subject to her husband. Yet even the husband remained subject to his own father, as long as his father was alive. The eldest father and husband, the patriarch, was head of the whole household, which included people, animals, land and other property. The patriarch might be something like the mayor of a town in our system of government. The operation of that whole patriarchal system depended on obedience within the family hierarchy. So to oppose one's parents was to threaten social disorder. In our terms such behavior would be insurrection or treason, punishable by death.

Adultery was another matter. For us, a married person, man or woman, commits adultery by having sex outside of the marriage. The offense is infidelity, betrayal of a trust or commitment, and it is against one's husband or wife. It is a personal offense. In ancient Israel, adultery was an offense only against the husband; it was an unlawful use of his property—his woman, his wife. More than a personal offense, it involved a financial loss: the man had paid his wife's father a bridal price for her, and she was important to the expansion of his family, the increase of his property.

Marriage and childbearing determined lines of ownership and inheritance in the patriarchal family. Property was passed on to the male children. Unlike the Romans, the Israelites did not recognize adoption as a basis for inheritance. It was important that the child born of a man's woman be his legitimate heir. But if someone else

44

had sex with a man's wife and she later had a child, whose child would it be? To what property was the child entitled? Similarly, if a man's new bride was not a virgin, how sure could he be that a child born through her was his own? A "used" woman was of no value to anyone.

Having sex with someone else's woman could cause serious financial and social problems. The "theft" involved was major. In ancient Israel, that offense was serious enough to be punished by death.

So merely knowing that a certain crime carried the death penalty does not say very much. The important question is, What really was the offense being punished and why was that offense considered so serious? In ancient Israel cursing one's parents and committing adultery had meanings very different from what those acts have in our culture.

Similarly, engaging in homogenital acts had a very different meaning. As we will see below, the sex itself was not the issue. Among the early Israelites, as Leviticus sees it, to engage in homogenital sex meant to be like the Gentiles, to identify with the non-Jews. That is to say, to engage in homogenital acts was to betray the Jewish religion. Leviticus condemned homogenital sex as a religious crime of idolatry, not as a sexual offense, and that religious treason was thought serious enough to merit death. Like a broken seal on a sterile medicine, an apostate disqualifies the whole people. The flaw must be corrected. The betrayer must be eliminated.

A Religious Consideration: Jewish Differentness

The condemnation of homogenital acts occurs in a section of Leviticus called "The Holiness Code." This list of laws and punishments spells out requirements for Israel to remain "holy" in God's sight. What does this mean?

According to Jewish belief, Israel was God's "chosen people" and was bound to God by a covenant, a pact. That covenant required that the Israelites not take part in the religious practices of the Canaanites, the people the Israelites had conquered "with God's help" and whose territory they had taken over as their own "Promised Land." To remain separate from the Gentiles, to be like the Lord God and not like other people, was to be "holy"—set apart, different, chosen, God-like, consecrated.

So a main concern of The Holiness Code was to keep Israel different from the Gentiles. Thus, chapter 18 of Leviticus begins, "You shall not do as they do in the land of Egypt, where you lived, and you shall not do as they do in the land of Canaan, to which I am bringing you. You shall not follow their statutes. My ordinances you shall observe and my statutes you shall keep, following them: I am the Lord your God."

The Canaanite religion included fertility rites—or, at least, that is how the Hebrew Testament portrays the matter. These ceremonies allegedly involved sexual rituals that were thought to bring blessing on the cycle of the seasons, the production of crops, the birth of livestock. Supposedly, during these rituals whole families and groups of families—husbands, wives, mothers, fathers, sons, daughters, aunts, uncles, brothers, sisters, cousins—all might have sex with one another.

Having sex with a menstruating woman and offering child-sacrifice to the Canaanite god, Molech, are other alleged Canaanite practices listed in this section of The Holiness Code.

The Holiness Code prohibits all those acts. It calls them all "abominations" and prescribes that "whoever commits any of these abominations shall be cut off from their people" (Leviticus 18:29). This same section of The Holiness Code includes the prohibition of male homogenital acts.

The point is that The Holiness Code of Leviticus prohibits male same-sex acts because of religious considerations, not because of sexual ones. The concern is to keep Israel from taking part in Gentile practices. Homogenital sex is forbidden because it is associated with pagan activities, with idolatry, with Gentile identity.

The argument in Leviticus is religious, not ethical or moral. That is to say, no thought is given to whether the sex *in itself* is right or wrong. All concern is for keeping Jewish identity strong.

Comparisons with Contemporary Experience

There used to be a church law that forbade Roman Catholics to eat meat on Fridays, and in some places the same requirement, now less strictly interpreted, still applies during Lent. That church law was considered so serious that violation was a mortal sin, supposedly punishable by hell. Yet no one believed that eating meat was something wrong in itself. The offense was against a religious responsibility: one was to act like a Catholic.

Or again, we sometimes hear of satanic rituals that include sexual acts. Jews and Christians today would certainly object to such sex. They would object even if the sex occurred between a married man and woman. Why? Not because a husband and wife have no right to share a sexual experience, but because that sex involves worship of the devil. Religious concerns, not sexual ethical ones, are the reason for the objection.

Those examples are parallels to the prohibition of male-male sex in Leviticus. Not sex, but violation of Judaism is what was prohibited.

The situation in ancient Israel was very different from our own. Except under unusual circumstances, sex in our culture plays no role in religious rituals. No sex today, gay or straight, has the religious associations to which Leviticus objected. So the Leviticus code is irrelevant for deciding whether gay sex is right or wrong. Though the Hebrew Testament certainly did forbid male homogenital activity, its reasons for forbidding it have no bearing on today's discussion of homosexuality.

47

What is an Abomination?

One last consideration confirms that interpretation. The Leviticus text says that it is an "abomination" for a man to lie with a man as with a woman.

Once again, in standard English, that sounds pretty bad. As one preacher vividly described it, an abomination is something that makes God want to vomit. But what does the word mean to the ancient Hebrew mind? There it's not as bad as it sounds to us.

Leviticus 20:25-26 suggests what "abomination" means. It reads:

> You shall therefore make a distinction between the clean animal and the unclean, and between the unclean bird and the clean; you shall not bring abomination on yourselves by animal or by bird or by anything with which the ground teems, which I have set apart for you to hold unclean. You shall be holy to me; for I the Lord am holy, and have separated you from the peoples to be mine.

Evidently, "abominable" is just another word for "unclean." An "abomination" is a violation of the purity rules that governed Israelite society and kept the Israelites different from the other peoples.

Certain animals were thought to be clean and so allowed to be eaten; and for differing reasons certain other animals—like pigs, camels, lobsters and shrimp—were thought to be unclean, not to be eaten. Likewise, certain practices that involved the mixing of kinds—like sowing a field with two different kinds of seeds or weaving a cloth from two different kinds of fibers or a man's having sex with another man as with a woman—were thought to be unclean and so were not to be done. Moreover, certain events, generally unavoidable—like menstruation in a women, seminal emission in a man, attending to a burial, giving birth—made a person unclean for a certain length of time.

It is difficult to recapture the meaning of "clean" and "unclean," "pure" and "impure," in ancient Israel. What was the rationale behind all those different instances of uncleanness? What made all those things abominations?

Some suggest that the Jewish purity rules were principles of sanitation, that certain things were forbidden because they were health hazards. But this suggestion presumes more medical knowledge than the ancients had, and the suggestion does not make complete sense of the purity laws. What is unhealthy about mixing cotton and linen in a fabric? Or cotton and polyester, for that matter?

Even in obvious matters of health, that suggestion does not pan out. For example, a person with certain skin diseases was considered "leprous"—not in today's technical sense of the term— and was declared unclean. But if the disease spread and covered the whole body, the person was no longer unclean: "since it has all turned white, he is clean" (Leviticus 13:13). Apparently completeness or consistency in a person, rather than disease or infection itself, provides some key to understanding Israel's notion of purity. But what sense does this make compared with what we now know about health and infection?

Whatever the rationale was behind the ancient Hebrew purity laws, such thinking certainly has nothing to do with ethics as we understand it. Indeed, such thinking is almost completely foreign to our own culture.

Contemporary Examples of Uncleanness

That is not to say that there is no concern for "clean" and "unclean" in our own day. We still do sometimes call things "dirty," and we mean disgusting and forbidden, just as the ancient Israelites did. But our reasoning is different. And even among ourselves, there is hardly anything that everyone would agree is "dirty" or "unclean." The following examples may at least provide a comparison with Israel's concern about cleanness and uncleanness.

Except for mixing up God in the matter, the preacher was on target when he said that an abomination, something dirty, makes you "want to vomit." What a culture considers dirty is usually something that makes its members uncomfortable. They feel funny, perhaps even feel sick. We learn what's "dirty" when we're little and people say, "Ugh! That's dirty!" "That's gross!" We learn to feel uncomfortable about things that the people around us don't like—like throwing food or soiling our pants or playing in the potty. Being "dirty" does involve uncomfortable feelings—and those feelings are learned.

Perhaps most people would agree that picking your nose and eating snot is gross and disgusting. Some might even say it's dirty, especially when talking to a child.

But just because it's dirty, just because people find it disgusting, does not mean it is wrong. In fact, eating snot is not even unhealthy. Mucus that is not removed from the nose just passes down the back of the throat and into the stomach anyway. Dirty and wrong do not necessarily go together—neither in our culture nor in ancient Israel.

In some societies people eat dogs, cats, snails, raw fish, ants or grasshoppers. To us that may be disgusting. It may seem gross or dirty. But it certainly is not wrong. It is just something with which *we* are uncomfortable.

In the early 1950s, styles were changing and women were just beginning to wear pants suits. Lots of women felt uncomfortable about that and even debated whether or not it was right. Should women wear pants outside the home or for shopping or even in church? From childhood they were taught how girls are supposed to behave. Though it was only custom they learned, they had never known anything else. Their custom seemed eternal decree, "the way it has always been." Some even argued, "God never meant for women to wear pants!" Custom was turned into the law of God. A matter of mere social convention was thought to be a matter of morality.

That same kind of thinking surrounded other issues as the styles changed: women smoking or driving cars, men wearing long hair or brightly colored shirts or earrings and other jewelry. What felt uncomfortable was taken to be wrong. Social taboo was turned into sin.

That same uncomfortable feeling and descriptions like "disgusting" and "gross" often also surround sexual matters. But talking about sex may be the one time when we still use the words "dirty" or "impure."

Supposedly, certain sexual words are dirty, and some people really are upset by them. But others just shrug all this off. With more frequent usage, the emotional impact of "dirty words" has worn off.

Similarly, many people are uncomfortable with sex, so children "pick up" from them that sex is "dirty." Many never get beyond the influence of those powerful feelings, learned early in life. They never appreciate the difference between what is supposed to be dirty and what is wrong. Especially where sex is concerned, for them "wrong" means that they feel funny about it.

Most people's attitude toward homosexuality is just like that. They feel funny about it, so they say it's wrong. Pressed to explain why it's wrong, they cannot come up with good reasons. They just squirm and screw up their face, seeming to say, "It disgusts me" or "I just don't like it." But "dirty" has to do with custom and feelings, not with well-reasoned ethical judgments.

The book of Leviticus calls male homogenital acts an abomination. That means it was considered unclean. The early Israelites thought it was dirty. It was prohibited not because it was wrong in itself but because it offended sensitivities. The Book of Leviticus associated those sensitivities with Israelite religion and made homogenital acts a ritual violation. So according to Leviticus male-male sex was abominable because it offended religious sensitivities. Homogenitality made a man like a Canaanite. And to the Israelites, God's chosen people, that was unacceptable.

A Hebrew and Greek Word Study

The very Hebrew term used in Leviticus conveys the meaning just explained. "Abomination" is a translation of the word *toevah*. This term could also be translated "uncleanness" or "impurity" or "dirtiness." "Taboo," what is culturally or ritually forbidden, would be another accurate translation.

The significance of the term *toevah* becomes clear when you realize that another Hebrew term, *zimah*, could have been used—if that was what the authors intended. *Zimah* means, not what is objectionable for religious or cultural reasons, but what is wrong in itself. It means an injustice, a sin.

Clearly, then, Leviticus does not say that for man to lie with man is wrong or a sin. Leviticus says it is a ritual violation, an uncleanness; it is something "dirty."

The conclusion of this little word study is no accident. It finds further confirmation in the Septuagint, the ancient Greek translation of the Hebrew Testament.

In the centuries before Christ, more and more Jews were living outside of Palestine. Many of them no longer understood Hebrew, but they did speak Greek, the common language of the Roman Empire at that time. So sometime between 300 and 150 B.C.E., a Greek translation of the Hebrew Scriptures was prepared so that Greek-speaking Jews could still read and study their Sacred Scriptures.

In the Septuagint, the Hebrew word *toevah* in Leviticus 18:22 is translated with the Greek word *bdelygma*. Fully consistent with the Hebrew, the Greek *bdelygma* means a ritual impurity, an uncleanness. Once again, there were other Greek words available, like *anomia*, meaning a violation of law or a wrong or a sin. That word could have been used to translate *toevah*. In fact, in some cases *anomia* was used to translate *toevah*—when the offense in question was not just a ritual impurity but also a real wrong or an injustice, like offering child sacrifice or having sex with another man's wife. The Greek translators could have used *anomia* to translate *toevah* in the case of "man lying with man." They could have—if that is what they intended. They did not use *anomia*; they used *bdelygma*.

Evidently, the Jews of that pre-Christian era simply did not understand Leviticus to forbid male-male sex because it is wrong in itself. They understood Leviticus to forbid male-male sex because it offended ancient Jewish sensitivities: it was dirty and Canaanite-like, it was unjewish. And that is exactly how they translated the Hebrew text into Greek centuries before Christ.

The Meaning of Leviticus 18:22

All the evidence points to the same conclusion. An analysis of The Holiness Code and its cultural context and a study of the Hebrew and Greek terms used in the Leviticus text both show that Leviticus 18:22 forbids male homogenital acts because of their cultural and religious implications. But Leviticus makes no statement about the morality of homogenital acts as such. This was evidently not a concern in the Hebrew Testament.

Therefore, it is a misuse of the Bible to quote Leviticus as an answer to today's ethical question, whether gay sex is right or wrong. Leviticus was not addressing this question. The concern in Leviticus, the cultural context of that text, and the meaning of male-male sex in ancient Israel are all very foreign to the present situation. Today's question and that in Leviticus are simply two different things.

Well then, does the Bible offer some positive teaching in its treatment on homogenital acts in Leviticus? Distilled through an historical-critical reading of the text, the biblical lesson is this: Appreciate the legitimate place of taboos in society. There is a difference between good taste and bad taste, between social propriety and grossness, between decency and indecency, between courtesy and rudeness. Recognizing and respecting this difference is important.

We avoid some behaviors not because they are particularly wrong in themselves but simply because they offend people. Picking one's nose, burping, or passing gas are obvious examples—in *our* culture. Saying "bad" words is another. In fact, no word is bad, though some words are vulgar or crude. Still, depending on the situation, every word can be used for good or for harm. If certain words are offensive to some people, it might be wrong to use them around those people—not because the words themselves are wrong but because offending people is wrong. What is taboo is not necessarily wrong; still, under certain circumstances it might be wrong to break a taboo.

This examination of homogenital acts in Leviticus provides a useful reminder. Rules of etiquette and courtesy and accepted social conventions are necessary for the harmonious functioning of society. Much of what we do or avoid in public depends on what is socially acceptable or unacceptable. To attend to this matter is part of being a virtuous person—or, said religiously, part of being a good Jew or a good Christian or a good member of any religion.

On the other hand, social conventions and taboos are always shifting and changing. Indeed, when conventions are misguided, unreasonable or oppressive, they ought to be changed, and change in these matters often entails heated debate and outright conflict. Thus, the late Twentieth Century is a time of unprecedented social upheaval. Despite it all, the important point is to recognize the difference between real wrong and mere taboo. Though it is not always easy to know the difference, we must not be hard-headed and treat as an ethical issue what is simply a matter of convention. Rather, with openness, intelligence, reasoned judgment, and good will we must continually work together to form a just, high minded and noble society.

Five. Purity Concerns in the Christian Testament

The Hebrew Testament forbids homogenitality for purity reasons. Male-male sex makes one unclean. It breaks a religious taboo. It associates one with the Canaanites. The Hebrew Scriptures also list other purity requirements—like washing at prescribed times or not eating certain foods.

The prime example of a religious requirement was the circumcision of all males. If a man was not circumcised, he did not qualify as a Jew. If he did not bear on his body the mark of the religion of Israel, he was not a member of God's chosen people.

But no one thought that God rejected the uncircumcised, that they could not be just and holy, that they could not enjoy God's approval. The prophets of Israel often praised the righteousness of Gentile people even while condemning Israelites for abandoning God's ways. Likewise, no one thought that non-Jews had to follow the dietary laws of the Jewish religion, though many Gentiles were

recognized as good people. Circumcision and the purity requirements of the Jewish Law were part of being a Jew. They were not
necessarily part of being a good person, just and righteous before
God.

Jesus' Teaching about Purity

Jesus knew that difference. He is very clear that being a good
person and keeping the requirements of the Jewish Law are not the
same thing. He is also very clear that the only thing that matters is
being a good person. One of the reasons that Jesus was killed was
because he challenged the real importance of the Law.
"Listen and understand," he said.

> It is not what goes into the mouth that defiles a person, but
> it is what comes out of the mouth that defiles. . . . What
> comes out of the mouth proceeds from the heart, and this is
> what defiles. For out of the heart come evil intentions,
> murder, adultery, fornication, theft, false witness, slander.
> These are what defile a person, but to eat with unwashed
> hands does not defile. (Matthew 15:10, 18-20)

In that way Jesus rejected the importance of the Jewish pu-
rity/uncleanness laws. The only purity that mattered for Jesus was
"purity of heart."

Being "Pure of Heart"

What does this "cleanness of heart" mean? Some people took
it to mean you were not supposed to have "dirty thoughts." You
were not supposed to be "impure" in your mind. Of course, "dirty"
and "impure" referred to sex: you were not supposed to think
about sexual things.
What a distortion of Jesus' teaching! Jesus was not preoccupied

with sex. He was concerned about being a good person, about being good to the core.

Jesus objected to external religious show—fasting so others can see, praying in front of everybody, putting a lot of money into the collection so others will notice. Jesus said, "Beware of practicing your piety before others in order to be seen by them. . . . Whenever you pray, go into your room and shut the door and pray to your Father who is in secret" (Matthew 6:1, 6). Jesus praised the widow who was able to put only the smallest of coins into the collection. He praised her because she gave from her heart (Mark 12:42-44).

Jesus insisted that virtue must go as deep as the heart. So in Mark 7:6, Jesus quotes the prophet Isaiah against those concerned about ritual washings: "This people honors me with their lips, but their hearts are far from me." Or when Jesus teaches about forgiveness, he says you must forgive others "from your heart" (Matthew 18:35). Or when Jesus teaches about sexual offenses against others, he says, "Everyone who looks at a woman with lust has already committed adultery with her in his heart" (Matthew 5:28). Jesus is not impressed with externals. He looks into the heart.

In summary Jesus says, "Blessed are the pure in heart, for they shall see God" (Matthew 5:8). For Jesus the "pure in heart" will see God, not those who are merely pure or clean according to the practices of the Jewish Law. Being a good person—honest, loving, just, kind, merciful, peaceful—is what matters before God. The purity requirements of the Law are no longer significant.

Early Christian Attitude Toward Purity

The early followers of Jesus held that same attitude. Chapter 15 of Acts of the Apostles—as well as many other places—records the debate in the early church about circumcision. Some claimed, "Unless you are circumcised according to the custom of Moses, you cannot be saved" (Acts 15:1). But the council of apostles and elders decreed that circumcision was not necessary. Thus, the early Christian church rejected a central requirement of the Jewish Law.

Peter, the leader of the twelve apostles, had come to that same conclusion regarding clean and unclean animals. In a dream, Peter

> saw the heaven opened, and something like a large sheet coming down, being lowered to the ground by its four corners. In it were all kinds of four-footed creatures and reptiles and birds of the air. Then he heard a voice saying, "Get up, Peter; kill and eat." But Peter said, "By no means, Lord; for I have never eaten anything that is profane or unclean." The voice said to him again, a second time, "What God has made clean, you must not call profane." (Acts 10:11-15)

Soon Peter realized the far-reaching implications of that revelation. He applied it to people, to Gentiles, saying, "God has shown me that I should not call anyone profane or unclean" (Acts 10:28). Peter explained himself with the same reasoning that Jesus used: "I truly understand that God shows no partiality, but in every nation anyone who fears God and does what is right is acceptable to God" (Acts 10:34). What matters is not ritual purity, not keeping the requirements of the Jewish Law, but justice and righteousness.

The apostle Paul also makes the same point over and over. He writes, "Circumcision is nothing, and uncircumcision is nothing; but obeying the commandments is everything" (1 Corinthians 7:19). Or again, "For in Christ Jesus neither circumcision nor uncircumcision counts for anything; the only thing that counts is faith working through love" (Galatians 5:6).

Echoing the teaching of Jesus, Paul says, "A person is a Jew who is one inwardly, and real circumcision is a matter of the heart—it is spiritual and not literal" (Romans 2:29). In this way Paul reinterprets what it means to be God's chosen people; it is a matter of the heart. He states boldly, "I know and am persuaded in the Lord Jesus that nothing is unclean in itself" (Romans 14:14).

That teaching summarizes a major theme in Paul's letter to the Romans. And, as we shall see, in order to make that very point, Paul mentions homogenital acts at the beginning of that letter.

Homogenitality in the Christian Testament

What does the Christian teaching about purity of heart say about homogenital acts? The single text in the Hebrew Scriptures that talks about homogenitality forbids it—but precisely because it is "unclean," not because it is wrong in itself. The Christian Scriptures insist that cleanness and uncleanness do not matter. Only whether you are doing good or evil matters.

Jesus and the Christian Testament reject the only biblical basis for condemning male-male sex. So we should expect no condemnation of homogenitality in the Christian Scriptures, or, if there is such a blanket condemnation, we should expect it to include some new reason for the condemnation. We should expect the Christian Scriptures to show that something about homogenitality or homosexuality in itself is wrong—that is, harmful, unkind, destructive, unloving, dishonest, unjust or some such thing. Or else we should expect same-sex acts to be condemned only when they do include these other wrongs, only when the sexual expressions are abusive, hurtful, wanton or lewd, just as heterosexual acts would be forbidden for these same reasons.

How do those expectations square with what the Christian Testament actually says? Following an historical-critical reading, they square perfectly well. There is no condemnation of homogenital sex in and of itself in the Christian Testament—neither because of purity concerns nor other concerns. At the same time, the Christian Testament is concerned about outlawing the abuse and exploitation that might be part of same-sex acts. Analysis of the relevant texts supports these conclusions.

59

Six. The Unnatural in Romans: Socially Unacceptable

There is only one Christian Bible text that actually discusses homogenital acts at any length. It occurs in the first chapter of Paul's letter to the Romans. This is the famous text from which people get the notion that gay sex is "unnatural." This is also the text from which they argue that venereal diseases—and today, HIV disease—are punishment for homogenital activity. This may also be the only Bible text that mentions lesbian sex. But considering to whom Paul is writing, how he is making his point, and to what end, all these conclusions seem to be wrong.

Here is the text of Romans 1:18-32. Only verse 27 is a clear reference to homogenital acts, male homogenital acts, though verse 26 is said to refer to lesbian sex. To understand these verses, however, the context of the rest of this long passage is required. At critical points, the original Greek words are noted in parentheses. Reference to these will help explain the meaning of this passage.

[18]For the wrath of God is revealed from heaven against all ungodliness (*asebeia*) and wickedness (*adikia*) of those who by their wickedness suppress the truth. [19]For what can be known about God is plain to them, because God has shown it to them. [20]Ever since the creation of the world his eternal power and divine nature, invisible though they are, have been understood and seen through the things he has made. So they are without excuse; [21]for though they knew God, they did not honor him as God or give thanks to him, but they became futile in their thinking and their senseless minds were darkened. [22]Claiming to be wise, they became fools; [23]and they exchanged the glory of the immortal God for images resembling a mortal human being or birds or four-footed animals or reptiles.

[24]Therefore God gave them up in the lusts of their hearts to impurity, to the degrading of their bodies among themselves, [25]because they exchanged the truth about God for a lie and worshipped and served the creature rather than the Creator, who is blessed forever! Amen.

[26]For this reason God gave them up to degrading (*atimias*) passions. Their women exchanged natural (*physiken*) intercourse for unnatural (*para physin*), [27]and in the same way also the men, giving up natural (*physiken*) intercourse with women, were consumed with passion for one another. Men committed shameless (*aschemosyne*) acts with men and received in their own persons the due penalty for their error.

[28]And since they did not see fit to acknowledge God, God gave them up to a base mind and to things that should not be done. [29]They were filled with every kind of wickedness (*adikia*), evil, covetousness, malice. Full of envy, murder, strife, deceit, craftiness, they are gossips, [30]slanderers, God-haters, insolent, haughty, boastful, inventors of evil, rebellious toward parents, [31]foolish,

faithless, heartless, ruthless. [32]They know God's decree, that those who do such things deserve to die—yet they not only do them but even applaud those who practice them.

The "Unnatural": Out of the Ordinary

Paul's letter to the Romans raises a question about the "natural" and the "unnatural." He says men "gave up natural relations with women and were consumed with passion for one another." This is certainly a reference to homogenital acts. And the "women exchanged natural relations for unnatural." The Greek words translated as "unnatural" are *para physin*. What do these words mean?

Physis is the Greek word for nature. It is the root of the English word "physics," the study of the natural world. The adjectival form of the same word, *physikos*, occurs in the English word "physical." But as even English usage suggests, the word could be used in various senses.

What exactly did Paul mean when he used this word? This is not easy to say, but this much is clear: Paul did not use the word "nature" in our abstract sense of "Nature and the Laws of Nature." His usage was more concrete. For Paul, the "nature" of something was its particular character or kind. Consider some examples.

In Galatians 2:15, Paul speaks of those who are Jews by nature, and in Romans 2:27, he speaks of those who are Gentiles by nature (though the literal reference to the Gentiles reads "uncircumcision by nature"). It is difficult to make sense of this usage. Attempting to do so, the English translations in our Bibles omit any reference to nature and simply read "Jews by birth (*physei*)" and "those who are physically (*ek physeos*) uncircumcised," but the Greek word for nature occurs in both these passages. In Romans 2:14, Paul speaks of Gentiles who follow their own conscience and "do instinctively (*physei*) what the law requires," but the Greek text

63

reads "by nature," and the implication is that these Gentiles act as is consistent with the kind of persons they are. In Galatians 4:8, Paul mentions "beings that by nature (*physei*) are not gods," and his reference is to the powers or "spirits" which supposedly govern the universe. Or again, in 1 Corinthians 11:14, Paul writes, "Does not nature (*physis*) itself teach you that if a man wears long hair, it is degrading to him?"

In all those cases, Paul uses the term "nature" to imply what is characteristic or peculiar in this or that situation. You would not expect a Jew not to be a Jew or the uncircumcised not to be uncircumcised. That is, you would not expect someone raised as a Jew to be ignorant of the Jewish Law, and you would not expect a Gentile to act like a Jew; that is not their "nature." According to the standard practice of Paul's day, you would not expect men to wear long hair; that is not what "nature" requires (though it is obvious that Paul refers to custom and that "nature," as we understand the word, has nothing to do with the length of a man's hair). Once you knew the true God of the universe, you would not believe the forces of this world are divine; that is not to be expected, for by their very "nature" they are otherwise.

For Paul, something is "natural" when it responds according to its own kind, when it is as it is expected to be. For Paul, the word "natural" does not mean "in accord with universal laws." Rather, "natural" refers to what is characteristic, consistent, ordinary, standard, expected and regular. When people acted as was expected and showed a certain consistency, they were acting "naturally." When people did something surprising, something unusual, something beyond the routine, something out of character, they were acting "unnaturally." That was the sense of the word "nature" in Paul's usage.

The Greek word *para* usually means "beside," "more than," "over and above," "beyond." We retain this meaning in many English words. A paraprofessional is someone who is not trained in a particular field but who assists those working in that field. For example, "paralegal" refers to people who are not lawyers but who work with lawyers and other legal professionals.

In a handful of stock phrases, *para* can also mean "contrary to," so *para physin* could be translated "contrary to nature." But given Paul's own usage of these terms, the sense is not "in opposition to the laws of nature" but rather "unexpectedly" or "in an unusual way," what we might mean if we said: "Contrary to her nature, Jean got up and danced last night."

So what does it mean when Romans says that the "women exchanged natural relations for unnatural and the men likewise gave up natural relations with women and were consumed with passion for one another"? It means that these women and men were engaging in sexual practices that were not the ones people usually perform. The practices were beyond the regular, outside the ordinary, more than the usual, not the expected.

There is no sense whatever in those words that the practices were wrong or against God or contrary to the divine order of creation or in conflict with the universal nature of things. According to Paul's usage, the words only say that the practices were different from what one would generally expect. Rather than "unnatural," the words *para physin* in Romans would more accurately be translated as "unusual" or "peculiar" or "out of the ordinary" or "uncharacteristic."

Even God Acts "Unnaturally"

A study of the Greek words suggests that there is no ethical condemnation in Paul's use of *para physin*. This conclusion seems certain. Why? Because there is further evidence on the matter, and that evidence is weighty.

In Romans 11:24, Paul uses those very same words to talk about God. Paul describes how God grafted the Gentiles into the olive tree that is the Jews. Now Jew and Gentile are one in Christ. But to graft a wild tree into a cultivated tree is not the ordinary thing to do; it is something unusual. Still, that is what God did through Christ.

In Paul's understanding of the words, God himself acted *para physin*. God did what was "unnatural." God behaved "in an unusual way."

If to act *para physin* is immoral, then God must be immoral—and that is patently absurd. Therefore, there can be no moral meaning in those Greek words for Paul. Once again the conclusion emerges: Romans is not a moral condemnation of male-male sex.

Other Opinions about *para physin*

There is considerable debate on this matter. Some biblical scholars insist that *para physin* does mean "unnatural" or "contrary to nature" and understand "nature" in the abstract sense of "Nature and Nature's Laws." The term *para physin* was used in Stoic philosophy, which pervaded the Roman Empire in Paul's day, and by then Stoic philosophy was well on its way to developing a notion of natural law built into the universe.

We use the words "stoic" or "stoical" today to mean unfeeling, unmoved by emotion, austere, rigidly disciplined. This popular meaning comes from Stoic insistence that all things are governed by a law built into nature and that human reason can discern that law. Virtue consists in living by reason, not by emotions or feelings.

When applied to sex, this philosophy said that the purpose of sex is procreation, so any use of sex for mere pleasure violates its core nature. Any non-procreative sex was called *para physin*. Homogenitality—and other sex acts, like heterosexual intercourse during the woman's period—fell into this category. Sex that could be procreative was called *kata physin* or "according to nature." Thus, when the world of Paul's day spoke of sex *para physin*, the reference might be homogenital acts.

Paul was certainly aware of that terminology. He could hardly have lived in the Greek-speaking world of his day without picking up some Stoic thought. Indeed, in the very passage of Romans under consideration here, Paul speaks of "things that should not be done" (1:28). The Greek is *ta me kathekonta*, and this is another standard Stoic formula.

Some biblical scholars go so far as to suggest that in this passage Paul integrates Stoic thought about natural law with Jewish and Christian thought about God's creation of the world. For Paul refers to the Creator, and Paul faults the Gentiles for worshiping images of humans, birds, beasts and snakes. So these scholars conclude that Paul had in mind the Genesis account of creation of the world and of all the animals as well as the role of Adam and Eve, man and woman, as part of God's plan. They argue that Paul sees homosexuality as a violation of this plan, as the subversion of the natural order built into the created universe.

However, the more common opinion is that only Wisdom 13:1-9, and not Genesis, is behind Paul's argument in Romans 1:18-23. The theme in Wisdom closely parallels Paul's criticism of the Gentiles. They ought to know God from all that is created, but they foolishly worship idols instead. Moreover, to find a case about sexual orientation in Genesis is clearly to read into that ancient text a twentieth-century concern. More on this in Chapter Eight.

The key question in this debate is whether to read Paul on his own terms or in terms of Stoic philosophy. Though Paul certainly knew some technical Stoic terms and even uses them in this section of Romans, close attention to how Paul uses them suggests he ignores their technical meaning—if he even understood it.

Clearly, Paul does not use the term "nature" the way the Stoics did. Paul's usage is concrete; the Stoic usage is abstract. Moreover, although Paul is aware that sex *para physin* would refer to non-procreative sex, including same-sex acts, he certainly is not concerned about procreation. Paul was expecting the speedy return of Christ, the end of the world, so nowhere in his writings does he show concern for procreation.

Finally, in Romans 11:24, Paul seems to take the Stoic terminology and throw it to the wind. Paul uses the analogy of grafting
cuttings into a stock. He writes to the Gentiles about the Jews as
follows: "God has the power to graft them in again. For if you have
been cut from what is by nature [*kata physin*] a wild olive tree and
grafted, contrary to nature [*para physin*], into a cultivated olive
tree, how much more will these natural [*kata physin*] branches be
grafted back into their own olive tree." Paul seems deliberately to
play with the Stoic terms *kata physin* and *para physin*. And he
mangles them. In Paul's mind, it seems, to speak of "natural" or
"unnatural" in the face of God is to speak foolishly. Those prescrip-
tions have no hold on the power and mercy of God.

Do not miss the point here. It is not that he is opting for a
miraculous, rather than a down-to-earth approach to religion. It is
not that Paul is rejecting natural-law theory. The point is that Paul
simply did not understand such theory. Paul was simply not using
these words as the Stoics did. If he were, he could not and *would
not* have portrayed God acting "contrary to nature."

Therefore, Paul is not to be understood in terms of Stoic philosophy. If he is understood on his own terms, it becomes clear that
Paul is merely being the good preacher. He knows how to work his
audience. A preacher today might quote the first line of a rock song
to get the attention of the teenagers, though the preacher does not
follow popular music and could not really say what the song is
about. Likewise, Paul throws around the terminology of the day to
impress his Roman readers. He wants to identify with them and
win a hearing. He becomes all things to all people so that he might
save at least some (1 Corinthians 9:22). But the technical Stoic
meaning of his terms does not constrain his meaning. To be sure,
Paul was an urbane citizen of the Roman Empire. But he was a Jew
at heart, not a Stoic. And his Jewishness, more than his urbanity,
explains his discussion of same-sex acts in Romans.

A list of other considerations, which confirm this conclusion, unfolds below. Paul's Jewish mind on this matter is very different from

what the Stoic terminology would suggest.

What about Lesbian Sex?

The words *para physin* actually occur in verse 26. It talks about women who "exchanged natural intercourse for *unnatural.*" Is this a reference to female same-sex acts? Many have thought so.

Undoubtedly, one reason people think verse 26 refers to lesbian sex is because it mentions "unnatural" sexual relations, and, as the term is used today, "unnatural sex" means homogenital acts. Moreover, this is what the Stoic term of Paul's day could also mean.

But, as we have seen, Paul does not use the words *para physin* in the strict Stoic sense. Even if Paul knew those words could be used to refer to same-sex acts, the implication of those words for him was not the same as for the Stoics. According to the evidence in Paul's own writings, for him *para physin* simply meant something outside the ordinary.

So the reference to female sexual relations that are "beyond the ordinary" could mean many things. It might mean sex during menstruation, sex with an uncircumcised man, oral sex, heterosexual anal sex, having sex while standing up, or anything that would not be considered the standard way of having sex. In our own day, for example, some people would consider anything except the "missionary position" out of the ordinary. There is no need to read homogenitality into the *para physin* of verse 26. In Paul's usage this phrase could mean several different things. And if these sexual acts were non-procreative, they would qualify as *para physin* in the Stoic sense of the term, too.

There is another reason people might think verse 26 refers to female same-sex acts. The word "likewise" or "in the same way" links verse 26 with verse 27 and verse 27 clearly refers to male homogenital acts. That "in the same way" sets up a parallel between what the women do and what the men do.

69

But is the parallel that both the women and the men perform same-sex acts? Or is the parallel simply that both the women and the men gave up the expected way of having sex for something else, whatever it might be?

The latter explanation makes perfectly good sense of the text. The men and the women could both be involved in something "beyond the ordinary" without both being involved in homogenitality. Only if it is assumed that *para physin* means "unnatural" and that "unnatural sex" necessarily means homogenitality, does verse 26 have to refer to lesbian sex. But close attention to Paul's usage shows that those assumptions are very questionable. There is no need to read lesbianism into verse 26.

In fact, if verse 26 refers to lesbianism, some explanation is needed. Lesbianism was not a major topic of knowledge or discussion in the Greco-Roman world. We have only a handful of references to it in all the existing texts from the ancient world. Moreover, lesbianism is not mentioned anywhere else in the Christian Testament. Why in the world would Paul have brought up that subject and made an issue of it here? Why, if it is so important, is it never mentioned again?

There is also a further consideration, and it is the most telling. In verse 24, Paul introduces the topic of impurity. At issue is ritual violation of the Jewish Law. Under this topic Paul mentions what the women do and then what the men do. As will be shown below, this section of Paul's argument is precisely about uncleanness, not about sin. But the Hebrew Scriptures never mention female homogenitality. How could it fall under the Jewish heading of impurity? But something else, like sex during the menstrual period, could have qualified both as violating the Jewish Law and as non-procreative. Paul must have had something like that in mind when he spoke of the women doing sexual things *para physin* or outside the ordinary.

In any case, the burden of proof that verse 26 refers to lesbian sex certainly rests on those making that claim.

There is a lot at stake in the interpretation of this verse. If this verse does not refer to female homogenitality, then nowhere does the Bible even mention it, and condemnation of female homogenitality would have no biblical basis. What sense would the case against homogenitality make if only male, but not female, homogenital activity is to be condemned?

On the other hand, if the Bible nowhere condemns homogenitality in itself—as is the argument here—then the easier reading stands without problem: verse 26 does not refer to female same-sex acts but to some kind of heterosexual practices that were considered taboo, unusual or unclean, and were perhaps also nonprocreative. This interpretation seems the more reasonable.

But even if this interpretation is wrong, even if verse 26 is a reference to female same-sex acts, the general conclusion argued below must still apply: Romans may refer to same-sex acts, but it intends no ethical condemnation of them.

Social Disapproval, Not Ethical Condemnation

One more set of considerations supports that same general conclusion. In verses 26 and 27, Paul uses two words to describe the sexual acts he has in mind: "degrading passions" and "shameless acts." Neither of these words has an ethical connotation. Both refer simply to social disapproval.

Take "degrading passions," for example. The Greek word translated as "degrading" is *atimia*. It means something "not highly valued," "not held in honor," "not respected." "Ill reputed" or "socially unacceptable" also convey the sense of the word.

That is the very sense in which Paul commonly uses that word. For example, in 2 Corinthians 6:8 and 11:21, Paul applies that word to himself. He notes that he is sometimes held in disrepute or shame because of his commitment to Christ. Evidently, then, to be in *atimia* is not necessarily a bad thing.

Again, in 1 Corinthians 11:14 Paul uses the word to suggest

that it is "degrading" for a man to wear long hair. Even though, as we saw above, Paul says this is what "nature" teaches, it is clear that no ethical judgment is intended. Or again, in Romans 9:21 Paul speaks of clay pots fashioned "for dishonor." That is a polite way of talking about chamber pots, something people do not consider very nice.

In none of those cases does the Greek word express a moral judgment. So when Paul calls certain passions "degrading" in Romans 1:26, he is not saying they are wrong; he is merely saying they do not enjoy social approval.

Basically the same meaning applies to the word *aschemosyne*, translated as "shameless acts" in verse 27. Literally the word means "not according to form." You may recognize the English words "scheme" or "schematic" in the middle of that Greek word. The sense of the word is "not nice," "unseemly," "uncomely" or "inappropriate."

In 1 Corinthians 7:36 Paul uses that word to describe the father who refuses to give his daughter in marriage: that is not the socially correct thing to do. In 1 Corinthians 12:23, the prudish Paul refers to the "uncomely" or "unpresentable" parts of the body. Of course, he means the genitals.

Those references carry no weight of moral judgment. Likewise, then, in using those words Paul does not imply that male-male sex is wrong. He merely says it is not looked upon well. It is not considered nice.

Once again the same general conclusion arises. Paul uses certain words to describe male-male sex. A study of these words shows that he makes no ethical condemnation of male-male sex. He merely points out social disapproval of it.

A Convergence of Evidence

Without doubt, Romans does refer to homogenital acts. But equally without doubt, on an historical-critical reading, Romans makes no *ethical* condemnation of those acts. Both Paul's peculiar use of the term *para physin* and his use of *atimia* and *aschemosyne* to describe homogenital acts come together and support the same conclusion.

Why Bring Up Homogenitality at All?

If Paul does not think that homogenital activity is wrong, why does he say that it is uncomely and disreputable? And why would Paul ever say such things when he is writing to the Romans? Homogenital sex was an everyday part of their world. They thought it perfectly natural for men to be attracted to other men. While there was concern about some excessive and abusive practices, the Greeks and Romans saw nothing improper in such sex in itself. Why does Paul bring up the topic at all?

Social Disapproval and Jewish Uncleanness

Paul states there is something socially unacceptable about male-male sex. You may recognize here the same sense that we saw in the use of the word *toevah* in Leviticus. Translated "abomination," the meaning is "ritual taboo or impurity," something unacceptable for Jewish society. The word carries with it a sense of disapproval or improperness. Likewise, "dishonorable" passions and "shameless" acts in Romans carry that same sense of "inappropriate," "not socially acceptable."

The parallel with Leviticus seems to be deliberate. There were words, both Hebrew and Greek, that meant "ethically wrong." Those words could have been used in Leviticus 18:22 and 20:13, but, as we have seen, those words were not used. Similarly, Paul also had words that mean "ethically wrong," and he could have used them to refer to male-male sex. But he did not.

In fact, such words of ethical intent occur in that same first chapter of Romans. They occur before the section on homogenital acts, and they occur after the section on homogenital acts. But they do not occur within the section on homogenital acts.

In verse 18 Paul notes the "ungodliness and wickedness" of people who suppress the truth. These words translate the Greek *asebeia* and *adikia*. They mean something that is really wrong, unethical behavior, sin. This sense comes through even in the English translation. Then *adikia* occurs again in verse 29. With it there is a long list of things that are clearly wrong in themselves, wicked and evil, not just things that might offend people's sensitivity. Again, even the English makes that perfectly clear. And not one sexual offense occurs in that list.

Just as Leviticus deliberately called homogenital acts "unclean" but not sinful nor wrong, so Paul called homogenital acts socially unacceptable but not sinful nor wrong. Both Paul and Leviticus clearly intend to speak of homogenitality only as something inappropriate. The similarity here is real. And, although Leviticus talks of religious disapproval while Romans speaks only of social, the difference is not as big as it seems.

In the ancient Hebrew mind, religious uncleanness and social dishonor went hand in hand. This is clear in the Hebrew Scriptures. According to Genesis 34:14, it is *dishonorable* for Jewish women to be given to uncircumcised men. According to Ezekiel 22:10, a man who has sex with a menstruating woman *shames* her. In Ezekiel 28:10, the phrase "death of the uncircumcised" is a way of saying "a *disgraceful* death." And according to Job 36:4, cult prostitutes are considered to be *the lowest of the low* in society. In all these cases violation of purity laws also entails social disrepute. So the similarity between Leviticus and Romans is real, it is strong and it is deliberate.

Paul Raises a Purity Concern

Therefore, when he talks of homogenitality in Romans, Paul seems to have the Jewish Law in mind. He seems to regard homogenitality as dirty, an uncleanness, an impurity.

Is that the case? Is that why our interpretation of Romans has the same feel as Leviticus? Yes! Obviously so! Paul says as much in verse 24: God gave them up to *impurity* and to *dishonor*. Paul is making an issue over purity.

But why is Paul making a point of impurity? Jesus and Christianity are not concerned about purity; the Gentile Romans never did have such Jewish concerns. So why does Paul mention it?

The Two-fold Effect of Gentile Idolatry

Paul accuses the Gentiles of idolatry: they knew God but did not worship God. And what was the result of their idolatry? Paul says it was two-fold. It resulted in uncleanness and in real sin.

We have already seen that Paul uses two different kinds of words to describe the Gentiles' deeds. He calls their sexual deeds degrading, shameful, dishonorable. He calls their other deeds wickedness, evil, malice. The terminology itself shows a deliberate contrast between what is socially objectionable and what is ethically wrong. Paul has two categories of deeds in mind.

The structure of Paul's argument highlights that contrast in vocabulary. Three times Paul repeats the phrase, "God gave them up." This repetition divides his statement into different sections. Paul is arguing that, because they did not worship God, two situations resulted.

Paul begins verse 24 with "Therefore God gave them up in the lusts of their hearts to impurity." This statement introduces the first effect, impurity. But, as Paul often does, he digresses in praise of God. He catches himself and gets back on track in verse 26, repeating the catch phrase that structures his argument: "For this reason God gave them up to degrading passions." Then Paul talks of the first effect of Gentile idolatry: uncleanness in sexual matters.

In verse 28 Paul moves on to the second effect. He recalls his main argument: neglect of God brought these things on the

Gentiles. He begins verse 28 with "And." Evidently, he is introducing something new. This time he goes on to talk of evil, malice and real sins. He writes, "And since they did not see fit to acknowledge God, God gave them up to a base mind and things that should not be done."

Both the structure and the content of Paul's argument show that he has two different things in mind: uncleanness and real wrong. Not only did their idolatry lead the Gentiles into committing other ethical wrongs, real sins which do merit death, but because of their idolatry, God also "gave them up" to impurities, naughty conduct, shameful and disreputable things, like homogenital acts.

Well, that is a partial answer to the question. Paul mentions homogenital acts as an example of the impurity that is one effect of Gentile idolatry. Still, what is Paul getting at?

Disapproval of Male-Male Sex?

Is Paul disapproving of homogenitality, even though it is just an impurity? It certainly seems that way—at least for the time being. But watch what comes later. At this point Paul appears to be sympathizing with the common Jewish feeling that the Gentile culture is unclean, the Gentiles are dirty.

It sounds like Paul is taking part in a petty name-calling bout. He seems to be playing a game of we're-better-than-you. In fact, that's just what is happening. Paul is quoting Jewish prejudice precisely to counter and reject it. Paul will use that nasty rivalry between the Jews and the Gentiles to his own advantage.

Paul is appealing to Jewish self-righteousness. He is echoing the Jewish claim to moral superiority. Paul begins his letter to the Romans by allowing that both sin and uncleanness are the two-fold result of Gentile idolatry. And the Jews in Rome would certainly applaud him.

"The Due Penalty for their Error"

That understanding also explains another aspect of the Romans passage, and being able to explain that aspect strengthens the overall argument.

Verse 27 says that because men commit shameful acts with men they receive "in their own persons the due penalty for their error." There has been much debate about what this verse means. A very common understanding of this verse sees homosexuality as the error, and sexually transmitted diseases or even AIDS is supposedly the due penalty.

But that interpretation doesn't make sense. Heterosexuals also have sexually transmitted diseases, and if AIDS is God's punishment for homosexuality, God must love lesbians, for of all social groups they are least at risk for AIDS. Obviously, this text needs a better interpretation.

Besides, what is translated as "in their own persons" reads differently in the Greek. A better translation would be "among themselves." The reference is not to individuals and their persons but to the Gentiles as a whole, to their culture.

Moreover, the word "penalty" offers a loaded translation; it carries a negative connotation that is not in the Greek. The Greek word simply means "recompense," "reward" or "payment," which could be positive, negative or neutral.

Given what we already understand about the first chapter of Romans, a very easy explanation of verse 27 arises. The error Paul refers to is not homosexuality but Gentile idolatry. Idolatry is his concern throughout the whole of that chapter: they knew God but did not worship God. And the recompense that comes to the Gentiles because of their not worshipping God is the uncleanness that is a regular part of their culture.

Paul is saying that, in addition to committing real sin, the Gentiles are also soiled. Their culture is filled with unclean practices. Both sin and impurities abound among the Gentiles.

Paul's reasoning differs from what we generally think. We

would say that, because people sin, they are idolaters, they distance themselves from God. But Paul's Jewish heritage leads him to see this matter in reverse. Because people abandon God, wickedness abounds among them. For Paul the root of all evil is disregard for God. This idolatry, this turning from God, is the gravest of all human faults. For Paul and the Jewish religion, this is sin—and all the things we would call sin*s* are merely expressions of this core fault.

So wrongdoings and impurity are the result of Gentile idolatry, the result of their not worshipping God as the Jews do. Not acknowledging the Jewish God, they do not acknowledge the Jewish Law, so they do not share the Jewish purity rules. Therefore, they are unclean. The dirtiness of the Gentiles comes from their idolatry.

There it is, plain and simple. Rid the text of the prejudices that the Twentieth Century reads into it and all the pieces fall together. The text makes perfect sense. The only requirement is to recognize Paul's argument that Gentile idolatry has two very different results: sin and uncleanness. Paul raises the issue of homogenitality only as an uncleanness.

The Self-righteousness of the Jewish Christians

But the question still remains: why did Paul make a point of impurity again?

In fact, the issue was there all the while. Keeping or not keeping the Jewish Law was a hot issue of debate in early Christianity. The "Council of Jerusalem," as recorded in Acts 15, decreed that Gentiles converted to Christianity need not be circumcised nor keep the rest of the Jewish Law. But arguments and rivalries still went on. The issue was still quite alive.

For example, Paul wrote to the church at Corinth rebuking them for disputes during their common meals. Evidently, arguments over clean and unclean food were disrupting the Lord's Supper (1 Corinthians 8-11). Paul confronted Peter and "opposed him to his face" because Peter refused to eat with the Gentile Christians. Jewish Christians were putting strong pressure on Peter to keep the purity requirements of the Law (Galatians 2).

Many Jewish Christians still kept the Jewish Law, and they felt some sense of superiority because of that. Paul, of course, took the side of the Gentiles, teaching that faith in Christ and not fidelity to the Law is what justifies a person (Galatians 2:16). Paul was well known for his position.

Paul's Appeal to the Jewish Christians

So when Paul wrote to the Romans, he had quite a feat to accomplish. He intended to visit Rome, and he wanted the Christian church there to welcome him. But the Christians in Rome were like the Christians almost everywhere else: a mix of both Jewish and Gentile converts. Paul had to appeal to both sides without offending either of them, and they were often at each other's throats.

How did Paul handle the matter? Pretty shrewdly. He started his letter by addressing the Jewish Christians, and he played on their sense of superiority. Paul wanted to win the good will of the Jewish Christians. At first he would take their side. He said what they felt, what they might even boast, that the Gentiles are a dirty lot. He put the Gentiles down by pointing out their homogenital practices.

Ah, so that is where the question of homogenital impurity comes in!

But already by chapter two, Paul turns the tables on the Jewish Christians. He approaches the matter cautiously. At first he addresses them anonymously: "Therefore you have no excuse, O human being, whoever you are, when you judge another" (Romans 2:1). But by verse 17 it is clear that Paul is addressing no one other than the Jewish Christians: "But if you call yourself a Jew and rely on the law. . ."

So the Jewish Christians have their circumcision, and they avoid impurities. But, as Paul points out, their real sins still break the Law. They steal, commit adultery and rob temples. Therefore, the Jewish Christians have no right to boast about the Jewish Law. They have no right to look down on the Gentile Christians.

Paul hooks the Jewish Christians on their sense of superiority over the Gentile impurities, and then he reels them in. He undermines any sense of superiority the Jewish Christians might have. He disqualifies their self-righteousness over not engaging in dirty behaviors. Incisively he makes his point. In the face of faith in Christ and Christ's call for purity of heart, ritual behaviors and impurities do not matter. "A person is a Jew who is one inwardly, and real circumcision is a matter of the heart—it is spiritual and not literal" (Romans 2:29).

Paul's Appeal to the Gentile Christians

But Paul doesn't let the Gentile Christians off the hook, either. In Paul's mind and God's plan, the Gentiles come second. But Paul does eventually address them.

In chapter 9, Paul begins to turn attention to them, gently drawing them into the discussion. As he did with the Jews in Romans 2:1, at first he refers to them only indirectly, as "they" and as "the Gentiles." But by 11:13 Paul puts it to the Gentiles, addressing them directly: "Now I am speaking to you Gentiles." He rebukes them for thinking themselves better than the Jewish Christians, the first to be God's chosen people.

Homogenitality in the Overall Plan of Paul's Letter

Paul structures his letter to the Romans so that he can win the favor of both the Jewish and the Gentile Christians. He tries to appeal to both while keeping them in harmony with one another. He wants all to know the salvation that comes to everyone who has faith, "to the Jew first and also to the Greek" (Romans 1:16). That is his gospel: grace and peace to all from God and the Lord Jesus Christ (Romans 1:7). "For as in one body we have many members, and not all the members have the same function, so we, who are many, are one body in Christ, and individually we are members one of another" (Romans 12:4-5).

Paul's prayer is that the Christians at Rome "live in harmony with one another, according to Christ Jesus" (Romans 15:5). Paul does not want false issues to divide them, so he insists, "I know and am persuaded in the Lord Jesus that nothing is unclean in itself" (Romans 14:14).

Now Paul's reference to same-sex acts finally makes complete sense. Seen in the context of the whole letter to the Romans, that reference serves a rhetorical function. It is part of Paul's plan to win the good will of his Jewish Christian readers. Then he uses the same issue to make his point: the ritual requirements of the Jewish Law are irrelevant in Christ.

Why did he choose homogenitality and not some other purity issue? Why not talk about unclean foods or about circumcision? Well, from a twentieth-century point of view, the answer may sound crazy. But from a first-century point of view, it makes perfect sense: in those days homogenital activity was a safe topic.

Paul could not talk about clean and unclean foods because debate over foods was still splitting the Christian communities. Likewise, circumcision was still too sensitive an issue. But evidently homogenitality was not. It was an obvious point of difference, and apparently there was no argument over it.

The Jews were well aware that Leviticus forbade male-male sex only as an impurity; they would not say the Gentiles were sinning because of their homogenital practices. Paul's mention of homogenitality could let the Jewish Christians feel superior without, in anyone's eyes, accusing the Gentile Christians of real sin.

At the same time, the whole Gentile world was well aware of the Jews' peculiar attitude toward homogenital acts. The Gentiles just chuckled and shrugged the whole thing off. They would not be offended if Paul raised that issue in his letter. Besides, they knew that Paul was the "apostle to the Gentiles" (Romans 11:13). Surely, if anything, he was on their side.

So unlike other purity issues, homogenitality was the one that would work. With it, Paul could do what he needed to do in writing to the Romans:

- first gain the sympathy of the Jewish Christians by seeming to side with their prejudices;
- next show that the Jewish Christians were as guilty as anyone else in breaking the Jewish Law;
- then argue that in Christ the Jewish Law was superseded and that, above all, purity issues in the Law do not matter;
- and thus incline the Jewish Christians to better acceptance of the Gentile Christians;
- and finally rebuke the Gentile Christians sharply for any smugness they might by then be feeling.

The mention of homogenitality, Gentile "dirtiness," becomes a clever rhetorical ploy in Paul's presentation of "the gospel of God" (Romans 1:1).

Another Confirmation of the Same Conclusion

In Romans, homogenitality serves merely as an instance of Gentile "uncleanness," judged by Jewish standards. Paul introduces this "uncleanness" precisely to make the point that such matters have no importance in Christ. This is clear from every consideration already presented. Moreover, only if that is really the case does the whole structure of Romans make sense.

This interpretation completely explains the reference to male-male sex in Romans. Attention to the terms in the passage, study of the argument of the passage and analysis of the whole letter converge on the same conclusion. The letter to the Romans certainly does not consider homogenital acts to be sinful. Indeed, the success of Paul's letter to the Romans depends on this being so.

A further conclusion follows. Not only did Paul not think homogenital acts are sinful; more than that, he seems to have been deliberately unconcerned about them. In his considered treatment of the matter, he teaches that in itself homogenital activity is ethically neutral.

The Sin that Paul Would Condemn

Once again, a sad irony surrounds this matter. There is a religious lesson to be learned.

A long-standing and naive reading of the Scriptures has led many sincere followers of Jesus astray. They oppose and oppress lesbian and gay people in the name of the apostle Paul. Bolstered by societal prejudice and zealous in their sexual self-righteousness, Christians have been misreading Paul's letter to the Romans and rejecting members of the Christian community because of it.

Yet to insure the unity of believers was a major reason for Paul's writing. Paul insisted on faith and love as the things that really matter in Christ. But by misunderstanding Paul's argument, people unwittingly rely on tastes and customs instead of the word of God. They argue about what's dirty or clean, dispute who's pure and impure, and pit heterosexual against homosexual. Thus, they divide and splinter the church over what does not matter in Christ. In God's name they foment hatred and fuel oppression and disrupt society at large. They commit a grave injustice, the very offense that Paul's letter meant to counter.

This is a sad state of affairs. It is unworthy of followers of Jesus.

83

Seven. 1 Corinthians and 1 Timothy: Abusive Male-Male Sex

Two other texts in the Christian Testament have something to do with homogenital acts, and they can be treated together. Their meaning depends on the translation of two Greek words—*malakoi* and *arsenokoitai*—and their translation is highly debated.

The upshot of this discussion is as follows: *malakoi* has no specific reference to homogenitality, but *arsenokoitai*, which occurs in two texts, is some kind of reference to male same-sex acts. Specifically, these texts condemn wanton, lewd, irresponsible male homogenital acts but not homogenital acts in general.

Wide Variation in Translations

In both texts those words occur in lists of sinners of various kinds. It is hard to determine what any words in a list mean because the words have no context to help suggest a meaning. All that can be determined in the present case is that the words refer to something evil. But to what?

In 1 Corinthians 6:9-10, the 1952 Revised Standard Version translates the two words as one. The result is as follows:

> Do not be deceived: neither the immoral, nor idolaters, nor adulterers, nor homosexuals (*oute malakoi oute arseno-koitai*), nor thieves, nor the greedy, nor drunkards, nor revilers, nor robbers will inherit the kingdom of God.

The 1977 version of that Bible translates those two words as "sexual perverts." The 1989 New Revised Standard Version translates the two words separately as "male prostitutes and sodomites."

1 Timothy 1:9-10 in that same 1989 translation reads as follows:

> the law is laid down not for the innocent but for the lawless and disobedient, for the godless and sinners, for the unholy and profane, for those who kill their father or mother, for murderers, fornicators, sodomites (*arsenokoitai*), slave traders, liars, perjurers and whatever else is contrary to the sound teaching. . . .

Various modern versions translate those words differently. *Arsenokoitai* is rendered as "homosexuals," "sodomites," "child molesters," "perverts" or "people of infamous habits."

Malakoi is rendered as "catamites," "the effeminate," "boy prostitutes" or even as "sissies." But until the Reformation in the Sixteenth Century and in Roman Catholicism until the Twentieth Century, the word *malakoi* was thought to mean "masturbators." It seems that as prejudices changed, so have translations of the Bible.

The Catholic Church's very recent New American Bible invites the same cynicism. It translated *arsenokoitai* as "practicing homosexuals." How amazing! A first-century text would now seem to teach exactly what Roman Catholicism began teaching only in the mid-1970s: to be homosexual is no fault, but to engage in homogenital acts is wrong. The attempt to nuance the translation is certainly understandable and welcome. Still, this translation reads a whole new worldview into the original Greek text, for there was no elaborated awareness of sexual orientation in the First Century. Even worse, "practicing homosexuals" includes women as well as men. But as we shall see, *arsenokoitai* certainly refers only to men. At the instigation of Dignity/USA, a support group for lesbian and gay Catholics and their friends, the editors of the New American Bible agreed to delete the term "practicing homosexuals." In its place in subsequent editions, the vaguer word "sodomites" will appear.

A Possible Conclusion

The variety of translations shows that this whole discussion is very tenuous. The interpretations presented below are all that scholarship can offer: "the best available opinion of the day." There is no real certainty about what these texts mean.

Given that fact, maybe the conclusion should be very simple: nobody really knows what these words mean, so to use them to condemn homosexuals is dishonest and unfair.

In light of the interpretation given to Romans above, that conclusion does seem warranted. If our longest biblical treatment of same-sex acts shows Paul indifferent to the matter, the benefit of the doubt about *arsenokoitai* should fall in the same direction.

But matters of sexual ethics could never be so simple. So the Christian Testament's overall teaching relevant to homogenitality seems understandably nuanced. The weight of the historical evidence requires a more complex conclusion, and we need to attend to the two Greek terms that lie at the heart of the debate.

Malakoi: The Sexually Loose, Wanton and Lewd

First, consider the term *malakos* (the plural is *malakoi*). It is a very common word. Literally it means "soft." It is said of clothing in Matthew 11:8; it could be used to describe warm butter. Applied to moral matters, as John Boswell suggests, it could mean "loose," "wanton," "unrestrained" or "undisciplined." This seems the most sensible translation for *malakoi* in that 1 Corinthians passage.

In contrast, L. William Countryman thinks that the lists of sins in 1 Corinthians 6:9 and 1 Timothy 1:10 parallel the list of the Ten Commandments. So he looks in *malakoi* and *arsenokoitai* for something related to both sex and money, linking the commandment about adultery with the next commandment about stealing. Thus, he holds to the older thought that *malakoi* means "masturbators"—but he would add an overtone of financial wastefulness. In that case, the colloquial English term, "jerk-off," would catch the sense of the Greek. It would refer to a person so devoted to personal pleasure (masturbation?!) as to lack financial responsibility and good sense. This interpretation seems strained.

Yet another scholar, Robin Scroggs, has tried to link the term *malakos* with a particular expression of homogenitality in the ancient world. He calls this type "the effeminate call boy." These would be free (not slave) youths who chose to offer themselves for male-male sex in exchange for money—and for the thrill of it. Mark Antony, famous for his later romance with Cleopatra, had indulged in such prostitution as a youth. As these men grew older and tried to preserve their youthful looks, they might style and perfume their hair, rouge their face, and remove facial and body hair. "Effeminate" was, indeed, an insult thrown their way.

But there is very little evidence—and it is forced—that the term *malakos* was specifically linked with this effeminate homosexual style. For *malakos* was also applied to heterosexuals who were wanton or loose. Besides, as a contrast with "virile" or "manly" in certain texts, "undisciplined" or "weak" would translate *malakos* as well as "effeminate."

So the conclusion accepted here is that *malakos* simply does not refer to same-sex activity. 1 Corinthians 6:9 uses *malakos* to make a general condemnation of moral looseness and lewd, lustful and lascivious behavior.

Various Interpretations of *Arsenokoitai*

Next, consider the term *arsenokoitai*. It is even more difficult to explain. 1 Corinthians is our earliest record of the word. It occurs in the Bible only there and in 1 Timothy. It is rare in other literature. So scholars are left guessing what it might mean.

The word is a compound of two parts, and they are easy enough to translate. *Arseno-* refers to men, male humans, plain and simple. *Koitai* comes from the word that means bedroom or bed and refers to "lying" with—that is, having sex with—someone. More precisely, it refers to the active partner in sexual intercourse, the one who penetrates.

So the literal English translation of *arsenokoitai* would be "man-lier," "man-sleeper" or, more graphically, "man-penetrator."

But when the two parts of the word are put together, it is not clear what the word means. Is "man" to emphasize the gender of the sexual agent: male? Or is "man" to indicate the object of the sexual act? That is, does *arsenokoitai* mean a man who has sex with others, or does it mean a man who has sex with men? In the first case the word would refer to a man who is the active partner in intercourse with anyone, female or male. In the second case the word would refer quite specifically to a man who is the active partner in a homogenital act. But from the word itself there is no way of telling for certain which of these two meanings—or what other meaning—might have been intended. Language is not always logical. In English the word "lady killer" means neither a lady who kills nor a person who kills ladies but a man who knows how to charm women.

Scholars differ on their interpretations. Boswell suggests that *arsenokoitai* refers to male prostitutes. They were available to have sex with either women or men.

Countryman also believes that *arsenokoitai* may refer to male prostitutes but specifically to prostitutes who cultivate the elderly so they might inherit their estates. The Roman poet Juvenal makes sport of one such heterosexual affair.

If *arsenokoitai* does refer to male prostitutes, the objection is not to having sex, whether with a person of the opposite or the same sex. The objection is to some specific form of male prostitution.

Scroggs proposes an interpretation that could also have something to do with prostitution but prostitution of a particular form and strictly between men. He takes *arsenokoitai* to refer to the active partner in male-male sex, but he believes that such sex always occurred between an older man and a young boy. So in his interpretation the sin is not male-male sex *per se* but child abuse, pederasty. As already noted, Scroggs takes *malakoi* to refer to the passive pederast partner, the soft and effeminate call boy. So, according to Scroggs, these two words constitute a pair, and the call boy and the child-abusing man are both condemned.

Without Scroggs' emphasis on male prostitution and pederasty, other scholars also commonly take *malakoi* and *arsenokoitai* to be a pair. This supposed pair of Greek words is said to condemn homogenital activity in general. This particular interpretation is found in the current, standard New Testament Greek dictionaries, which do not yet reflect the latest scholarship. Similarly, this interpretation was behind the translation in the revised (and now, on this point, re-revised) New American Bible: "boy prostitutes and practicing homosexuals." And this interpretation was behind the translation in the 1987 New Revised Standard Version: "male prostitutes and sodomites."

As already argued, there is no specific reference to homogenital activity in the term *malakoi*. However, it is likely that *arsenokoitai* does refer to some form of male homogenital behavior. The probable clue to explaining this obscure two-part Greek word is not found by exploring Greek usage. The clue is, rather, in the Hebrew usage! *Arsenokoitai* appears to be a literal translation of a Hebrew term.

Man-Lying-with-Man Revisited

Though the Greeks had many terms for the various aspects of male homogenital behavior, Hebrew had no word for it at all. Recall that Leviticus had to use the clumsy phrase, "the man who lies with a male the lying of a women." Note how the familiar word stems, *arsen-* and *koit-*, appear in the Septuagint Greek translation of this phrase: *hos an koimethe meta arsenos koiten gunaikos.* Moreover, in a shorthand form of this phrase, as a way of speaking of male same-sex acts, the rabbis began to use the Hebrew words *mishkav zakur* (lying of a male) or *mishkav bzakur* (lying with a male). Translated literally for the Greek-speaking Jews, the result could well be *arseno-koitai*, "man liers," "those who lie with a male."

In summary, the suggestion is this: the Greek-speaking Jews coined the term *arsenokoitai*. They created the term by translating literally the rabbis' shorthand Hebrew phrase into Greek. If this is the case, *arsenokoitai* relates to the prohibition of male same-sex acts in Leviticus 18:22 and 20:13, and it means men who have sex with men. A study of the few non-biblical places where this word occurs and a study of the earliest translations of the Christian Testament into Latin, Syriac and Coptic support this interpretation.

So, it seems, 1 Corinthians 6:9 and 1 Timothy 1:10 are repeating the prohibition in Leviticus 18:22.

Questions about *Arsenokoitai* in the Christian Testament

How very peculiar! What can we make of that?
Leviticus forbids male-male sex as an impurity according to the

Jewish Law. But Jesus and Christian teaching rejected purity concerns as a basis for morality.

In fact, as we have seen, Paul's Letter to the Romans makes that very point, using male-male sex itself as an example. But Paul also wrote 1 Corinthians; and 1 Timothy, though probably not written by Paul himself, follows the Pauline tradition. Then why do these letters condemn what Romans shrugs off?

Of course, throughout the Roman Empire, Corinth was notorious for its sexual depravity. Perhaps Paul's concern about Corinth was different from his concern about Rome. Or had Paul revised his thinking between writing to the Corinthians and to the Romans? But if so, what about 1 Timothy, written much later than Romans?

Those questions leave much to ponder, and we may never have the complete answers to them. The historical evidence is scanty. But if we can understand more precisely what *arsenokoitai* was referring to, we may at least be able to make some sense of the matter.

Using Lists of Sins

Recall that in both 1 Corinthians and 1 Timothy *arsenokoitai* occurs in a list of various sinners. Scholars are pretty well agreed that those lists are not Paul's own.

Note, for example, that in 1 Corinthians the list names sinners who are excluded from the kingdom of God. But the kingdom of God is simply not a theme in Pauline teaching. Besides, it is clear that Paul is not specifically concerned about any of the particular sins in the list. He does not go back to write at length about, or even mention, any of them.

Thus, it appears that Paul just borrowed stock lists from the culture at large. He is encouraging his readers to be good people, and he does that by reminding them of the evils of the day. He just repeats the list of wrongs that people generally decried in his society. A current example would be someone today talking about "drugs, guns, child abuse and breakdown of the family."

The point is that this list of sins is not Paul's own. It comes from some other source and reflects society at large. Then, to understand what was being condemned as *arsenokoitai*, we need to know what first-century critics condemned as male-male sex.

The Decadence of the First Century

When the Greeks wrote about male-male love, they extolled it as the highest form of affection. It included emotional attachment and deep concern, friendship and shared values, and commitment to a common task. Sex was not the main focus of the relationship. Virtue was. Even when the relationship involved an adult and a youth, as it often did, the older man was like a mentor to the younger one. He introduced the youth to culture and learning, and encouraged honorable behavior.

In the first-century Roman Empire, however, moral decadence was rampant. Social critics of the day decried the low life. Men sought out boys and other men for sex—the critics complained and supposed—as a novelty in the face of overly abundant female prostitution. There was too much sex all around—the critics lamented—and same-sex practices were the obvious sign of that. Men kept and abused slaves as objects of their lust. Attractive girls and boys were kidnapped and sold into sexual slavery. (This may be why "kidnappers" occurs next to *arsenokoitai* in the list of sins in 1 Timothy 1:10.) As was already noted, Robin Scroggs even argues that the whole "model of homosexuality" of the day was pederastic. That is, it always involved an older man and a young boy or youth. Scroggs' position seems too simple. Still, this much is clear: social critics of the day thought of exploitation, inequality, abuse and lust when they thought of male-male sex.

So that is what the first-century moralists were condemning when they objected to same-sex behavior: exploitation, inequality, abuse and lust. That is what the Greek-speaking Jews were

93

likewise condemning in Roman society. That, then, we must conclude, is what the term *arsenokoitai* condemns.

Translating and Interpreting *arsenokoitai*

When 1 Corinthians 6:9 and 1 Timothy 1:10 are understood in their cultural context, the problem of translating *arsenokoitai* into English is apparent. This one word bottles up a whole worldview, and it is not the worldview of our day. No simple translation, but only a broad explanation, can adequately express its meaning.

To say that those texts condemn "homosexuals" or "homosexuality" is incorrect. The problem is not just that one could be homosexual without engaging in homogenital acts. And the problem is not just that "homosexual" includes women while *arsenokoitai* certainly does not. The problem is bigger than that. To say "homosexual" implies a psychological and sociological understanding of sexual orientation that was foreign to the early Christian world.

Even to say that *arsenokoitai* refers to "sex-between-men" is not accurate. For in using this term, the first-century authors had particular abuses in mind, and not all sex between men includes these abuses.

The contemporary gay subculture has derogatory terms that apply to some of the abuses suggested by these biblical texts. "Chicken hawk" refers to men who take advantage of attractive, inexperienced, young gay men. "Slut" and "whore" are insulting names that refer to men who are wildly promiscuous and unrestrained in their sexual desire, men who will have sex with anyone they can "make." But these contemporary terms, though validly suggestive, are hardly appropriate biblical translations for the first-century *arsenokoitai*. These terms, too, are closely tied to their own cultural context.

Neither does the Bible's own circumlocution, "men lying with men," provide a satisfactory translation of *arsenokoitai*. For the

94

meaning of these words changed within the Bible itself, and the meaning has again changed in our day. Leviticus condemns "men lying with men," but an understanding of that whole text and its culture make clear that its condemnation applies to something irrelevant both to early Christianity and to most of our contemporary Western world. That something is ritual impurity, violation of the ancient Jewish taboos that surrounded a man's Jewish identity. Under the Greek term *arsenokoitai*, two texts in the Christian Testament reiterate the Hebrew condemnation of "men lying with men." But an understanding of these texts shows that these very same words apply to something very different again. That something is the abuse, exploitation and lust associated with male-male sex in the first-century Roman Empire. But, still again, that is hardly what the English words, "men lying with men," mean in the late Twentieth Century. Today this phrase suggests male homosexuality—which, according to contemporary scientific understanding, implies a normal variation in sexual orientation that inclines men to emotional and genital intimacy with each other.

It may not be altogether possible to say in a one- or two-word English translation what *arsenokoitai* really means. So, caught in a distorting time warp, the Christian Testament may ever continue to support homophobic and unchristian attitudes and behavior. Nonetheless, it is possible to state simply and with certainty what 1 Corinthians 6:9 and 1 Timothy 1:10 do not mean. Their use of the term *arsenokoitai* implies no blanket condemnation of homosexuality, nor even of homogenitality.

The Lesson of 1 Corinthians 6:9 and 1 Timothy 1:10

A contemporary statement of the positive teaching of 1 Corinthians 6:9 and 1 Timothy 1:10 regarding male-male sex would run as follows. Biblical opposition to prostitution, incest or adultery does not forbid male-female sex acts as such. What the Bible opposes throughout is *abuse* of heterosexuality. Likewise, the

95

condemnation of *arsenokoitai* does not forbid male homogenital acts as such. In first-century, Greek-speaking, Jewish Christianity, *arsenokoitai* referred to exploitative, lewd and wanton sex between men. This, and not male-male sex in general, is what the term implied. This, then, and not male-male sex in general, is what these biblical texts oppose.

Across the board in sexual matters, the Bible calls for mutual respect, caring and responsible sharing—in a loaded word, love. The violation of these, but not sex in general, is what the Bible condemns. The lesson in 1 Corinthians 6:9 and 1 Timothy 1:10 is that this principle applies equally to hetero- and homosexuality.

Eight. Other Supposed References to Homosexuality

There are a number of other texts in the Bible that are sometimes said to refer to homosexuality, and there is an argument against homosexuality based on the Bible's positive teaching about sex. None of these is really part of biblical teaching on homosexuality. But to make clear why this is the case, this chapter will briefly consider these matters.

The "Alien Flesh" in Jude

The most debated of those texts is verse 7 in the short, one-chapter letter of Jude. Except for a few who continue to insist that the sin of Sodom was male-male sex, Scripture scholars today simply do not see homogenitality in this text. Nonetheless, like any vague text in the Bible, people can take it to mean what they want, and some modern translations encourage misinterpretation.

Jude faults the people of Sodom for lusting after "strange" or "alien" flesh. That is clearly what the Greek says—*sarkos heteras.* The King James translation of the Bible accurately presents this meaning:

> "Even as Sodom and Gomorrah and the cities about them in like manner, giving themselves over to fornication, and going after strange flesh, are set forth as an example, suffering the vengeance of eternal fire" (Jude 7).

What is this thing about "alien flesh"? It refers to humans having sexual intercourse with angels.

Verse 6 of Jude alludes to such a story, quite obscure, in Genesis 6:1-4)"the sons of God saw the daughters of men were fair; and they took to wife such of them as they chose." Verse 7, referring to Sodom, is meant to offer a similar story. You will remember that the "men" who visited Sodom were really angels sent from God. So the strangeness of the intercourse here does not refer to same-sex relations but to sex between angels and humans.

Moreover, an early Jewish tradition about the story of Sodom— evident in the non-biblical Book of Jubilees 7:20-21 and 20:5-6— suggests that the *women* of Sodom wanted to have sex with the angels staying in Lot's house. If this tradition is behind the letter of Jude, it is not likely referring to same-sex acts at all—neither between humans nor between a man and an angel.

So what should we make of this text? Understandably, we might want to know more about the fascinating notion of sex with celestial beings. The movie *Cocoon* successfully played on this very theme. But actually, there is not very much to tell. This text is irrelevant to our real-world situation and to our question about homosexual love. However, this text does provide an excellent example of how different the biblical worldview was from our own.

This text is also an excellent example of how translation can make the Bible say what it never intended. Of course, translators try to make the English rendition make sense to the reader. But sometimes what the Bible actually says just does not make sense in the modern world. A case in point is the present one. The 1989 New Revised Standard Version says Sodom "pursued unnatural lust," and the New American Bible says "practiced unnatural vice." The Jerusalem Bible says Sodom was "equally unnatural." Now, there is nothing in the Greek text that should be translated "unnatural." In current usage "unnatural sex" refers to homogenitality. So deliberately or not, such translations foster anti-homosexual sentiment. These translations are downright misleading. They are an embarrassment to modern Scripture scholarship. In this case, the vague but accurate King James translation, "going after strange flesh," deserves a tip of the hat.

Some Other Irrelevant Texts

2 Peter 2:6 mentions Sodom and Gomorrah in a list of examples of God's punishment: "by turning the cities of Sodom and Gomorrah to ashes [God] condemned them to extinction and made them an example of what is coming to the ungodly."

The text does not say what the ungodliness in question was. But because the text mentions Sodom, some have concluded the sin was homosexuality.

Hardly anyone at all would hold that opinion today. The point of the text is that God punishes the wicked. Sodom is simply listed as an example. There is no reference to any sexual offense here. This text does not specify what the sin in question was.

If a particular sin has to be specified, scholars would bet on sex with angels. For verse 4 introduces this matter when it begins, "For if God did not spare the angels when they sinned . . ."

Then we are back to the weird discussion we saw in Jude 7. The concern is sex between humans and angels. The matter is foreign to our worldview.

* * *

99

In a number of texts in the Hebrew Testament, the King James Bible mentions "sodomites": Deuteronomy 23:17; 1 Kings 14:24, 15:12, 22:47; 2 Kings 23:7. In this case, the King James translation gets an "F."

The Hebrew term here is *qadheshim*. Literally it means "holy" or "sacred ones." Recall that the Hebrew sense of "holy" also included the notion of "separated" or "set apart." Thus, as God's chosen people, Israel was to be "holy," that is, singled out and kept distinct from the Gentiles. So an equally valid translation for *qadheshim* is "devoted" or "dedicated ones." Of course, the dedication was to the gods and to service in their shrines.

Though hard evidence on the matter is almost non-existent, scholars have suggested that this term refers to male temple prostitutes, supposedly available for ritual sex acts with both women and men. So modern translations read simply "cult prostitutes," "temple prostitutes" or "male temple prostitutes." But there is still debate among scholars whether sexual rituals really did play a part in Canaanite rites, as the Hebrew Scriptures claim.

In any case, the sin in question was not any kind of sex act. The "devoted ones" were in the service of alien gods. The sin in question was idolatry. This is clear, for example, in the Bible's comment about King Josiah. The Second Book of Kings praises him for restoring the temple, renewing the covenant with the Lord, and ridding the temple of all remnants of foreign religion. Among other things, the king "broke down the houses of the male temple prostitutes that were in the house of the Lord, where the women did weaving for Asherah" (2 Kings 23:7).

There is no concern about homogenital acts in these texts. Only mistranslation would suggest that.

Adam and Eve, not Adam and Steve

All the above considerations show that the Bible nowhere condemns same-sex acts in themselves. Nonetheless, the question can still be raised, But what does the Bible advocate? What is the Bible's positive teaching?

Some people choose to shift the emphasis to that other question. They point out that the Bible speaks about heterosexual relations wherever it speaks positively about sex. They conclude that, despite any interpretation of isolated texts on homogenitality, the Bible's overall attitude still does condemn same-sex acts. As one wag cutely phrased the matter, "God created Adam and Eve, not Adam and Steve."

That argument may have emotional appeal, but it certainly is not valid. A number of considerations show this to be so.

Consider Adam and Eve and the story of creation. What was the point of those first two chapters of Genesis? The point wa to present a picture of our world in its sad and sinful state and to insist that this situation was not God's doing. God created a good world of beauty and pleasure. But people misuse creation, so life becomes hard and goes sour.

Genesis is a lesson in religion, a lesson about God's way and our sin. Genesis makes its point by presenting a story, and the story involves an example. The example is the case that is by far the most common in human experience: the man, the woman, their relationship with one another, and the children they may beget. The biblical author merely presents the standard case within ancient Hebrew life. What better example would one use to make a point?

But the story is only the vehicle for conveying the religious point. The story of Adam and Eve as such is incidental to the point. Genesis is not a lesson on sexual orientation. Nothing in those two chapters suggests that heterosexuality, in contrast to homo-sexuality, was a concern in the author's mind. To read that twentieth-century concern into the text is simply to misuse the Bible. A similar analysis applies to the other Bible texts about the love of woman and man for one another.

Furthermore, the Adam-and-Eve-not-Adam-and-Steve argu-ment depends on a logical fallacy—the *ad ignorantiam* argument,

argument by appeal to the unknown, argument based on assumptions about what was *not* said. The argument runs like this: since the Bible does not actively support homosexuality, it must be that the Bible condemns it. But this conclusion does not logically follow. What would follow is simply that we do not know the biblical mind on the subject.

Consider other examples where the point is much more obvious. You've heard a friend speak often and enthusiastically about his only brother, but you never heard him talk about a sister. Suppose you conclude that he has no sister or that, if he does, he certainly dislikes her. How valid is your conclusion? It is not valid at all. You know nothing about his sister nor about his special love for her. All you do know is what he happened to say about his brother.

Or again, the Bible often speaks about dogs but mentions cats only once, as roaming Babylonian temples, in Baruch 6:22. Should you conclude that the Bible is opposed to cats, and begin ridding your neighborhood of them? How valid would your position be? It is totally invalid. You know nothing about the Bible's attitude toward cats. The Bible hardly mentions them.

An endorsement of heterosexuality would imply a condemnation of homosexuality only if the two were mutually exclusive, an either-or choice. In that case, approving of one would mean condemning the other. But such a choice is not realistic. If it is real at all, it is only real in the minds of those making that argument. Obviously, then, their opinion does not depend on the Bible. On the contrary, their reading of the Bible depends on their personal opinion.

The fact that the Bible speaks often and positively about heterosexual relationships in no way implies a condemnation of homosexual ones. This is all the more obvious since the Bible does, in fact, speak outright about homogenitality in five places, and those references intend no blanket condemnation.

Biblical Endorsement of Homosexual Relationships?

Some scholars push the discussion to its opposite pole. Rather than merely agreeing that the Bible does not condemn homogenital acts as such, these scholars point out positive accounts of lesbian and gay relationships in the Bible.

The clearest example is the love of Jonathan and David. In a number of incidents, the First Book of Samuel suggests a deeply emotional relationship between these biblical heros.

For example, 1 Samuel 18:1-4 recounts a striking show of affection on the part of the prince, Jonathan, toward the ruddy and handsome shepherd boy, David, newly come to court:

> The soul of Jonathan was bound to the soul of David, and Jonathan loved him as his own soul. . . . Jonathan made a covenant with David, because he loved him as his own soul. Jonathan stripped himself of the robe that he was wearing, and gave it to David, and his armor, and even his sword and his bow and his belt.

King Saul's angry outburst against Jonathan in 1 Samuel 20:30 is also revealing: "You son of a perverse, rebellious woman! Do I not know that you have chosen the son of Jesse [i.e., David] to your own shame, and to the shame of your mother's nakedness?" Saul insults Jonathan in two ways. First, by slandering his mother as a "perverse, rebellious woman," the outraged Saul calls his own son, Jonathan, a bastard. But second, Saul disparages Jonathan's relationship with David. The Hebrew of this verse is ambiguous and, following the Greek Septuagint translation, could also be rendered, "Do I not know that you are an intimate companion to the son of Jesse?" Then, given that the words "shame" and "nakedness" are common biblical ways of talking about sex, surely the innuendo here is sexual. It appears that Saul is deriding Jonathan's sexual liaison with David, a matter about which Saul and his whole court would have easily known. So, in contemporary terms, Saul's second insult is to call his son a faggot. At stake in this whole intrigue, of course, is rivalry over the throne of Israel.

Moreover, at their parting, Jonathan and David demonstrate an intense sorrow:

> David rose from beside the stone heap and prostrated himself with his face to the ground. He bowed three times, and they kissed each other, and wept with each other; David wept the more. Then Jonathan said to David, "Go in peace, since both of us have sworn in the name of the Lord, saying, 'The Lord shall be between me and you, and between my descendants and your descendants, forever.'" He got up and left; and Jonathan went into the city. (1 Samuel 20:41-42)

Finally, at Jonathan's death David concludes his lament with this crescendo: "I am distressed for you, my brother Jonathan; very pleasant have you been to me; your love to me was wonderful, passing the love of women" (2 Samuel 1:26).

Could the relationship between David and Jonathan have been only a deep and faithful friendship? Perhaps. But their relationship has important parallels to that of Gilgamesh and Enkidu, commonly thought to be homosexual, in the ancient Sumerian epic. That is to say, their relationship fits the model of noble military lovers, common throughout the societies of the ancient mid-East, where Israel lay. Such male-male sexual relationships were so taken for granted that they would not have had to be noted explicitly. Besides, even modern Westerners must sense something more than simple friendship in the story of David and Jonathan.

Another case is the story of Ruth and Naomi. The Book of Ruth relates the very unusual commitment between the Jewish woman Naomi and her Moabite daughter-in-law Ruth. After the death of her husband, in contrast to the customs of the day and unlike her sister-in-law, widowed Ruth remains with Naomi. Ruth declares to Naomi, "Where you go I will go, and where you lodge I will lodge;

your people shall be my people, and your God my God. Where you die, I will die—there will I be buried" (Ruth 1:16-17). This pledge of love and commitment is so impressive that the passage is often read at contemporary heterosexual marriages. Few people realize that this statement was made by one woman to another.

Given how little is known about the women's world in antiquity in general and how little evidence we have about Ruth and Naomi in particular, it is impossible to say whether or not they shared a sexual relationship. In antiquity women had their own world, significantly segregated from men, but under male domination, it is not unreasonable to suppose that they often found support and affection among themselves.

The Book of Daniel offers a third case. Daniel 1:9 reads, "Now God allowed Daniel to receive favor and compassion from the palace master." Another translation reads, "By the grace of God Daniel met goodwill and sympathy on the part of the chief eunuch." This text could also be translated to read that Daniel received "devoted love." Moreover, there is some serious speculation that the servants at court or the "eunuches" in the ancient mid-East were not necessarily castrated men but rather homosexual men. For this reason they could be trusted around the harem. So some people suggest that Daniel's role in Nebuchadnezzar's court included a homosexual liaison with the palace master. The romantic connection would explain in part why Daniel's career at court advanced so favorably.

Were Daniel and Nebuchadnezzar's chief eunuch really lovers? Were Ruth and Naomi? Or were Jonathan and David? In the case of Jonathan and David one could impressively argue, Yes. But in the end, we simply do not have the historical evidence to answer with certitude one way or the other. Here, as elsewhere in the Bible, homosexuality remains an open question. Still, the real possibility of homosexual relationships in the lives of important biblical characters suggests that the Bible may be more open to same-sex love than most ever imagine.

Nine. Summary and Conclusion

The literal approach to the Bible claims not to interpret the Bible but merely to take it for what it obviously says. The words of the Bible in modern translation are taken to mean what they mean to the reader today. On this basis the Bible is said to condemn homosexuality in a number of places.

But an historical-critical approach reads the Bible in its original historical and cultural context. This approach takes the Bible to mean, as best as can be determined, what its human authors intended to say in their own time and in their own way. Understood on its own terms, the Bible was not addressing our current questions about sexual ethics. The Bible does not condemn gay sex as we understand it today.

The sin of Sodom was inhospitality, not homosexuality. Jude condemns sex with angels, not sex between two men. Not a single Bible text clearly refers to lesbian sex. And from the Bible's positive teaching about heterosexuality, there follows no valid conclusion whatsoever about homosexuality.

Only five texts surely refer to male-male sex, Leviticus 18:22 and 20:13, Romans 1:27 and 1 Corinthians 6:9 and 1 Timothy 1:10.

All these texts are concerned with something other than homogenital activity itself, and these five texts boil down to only three different issues.

First, Leviticus forbids homogenitality as a betrayal of Jewish identity, for supposedly male-male sex was a Canaanite practice. The Leviticus concern about male-male sex is impurity, an offense against the Jewish religion, not violation of the inherent nature of sex. Second, the Letter to the Romans presupposes the teaching of the Jewish Law in Leviticus, and Romans mentions male-male sex as an instance of impurity. However, Romans mentions it precisely to make the point that purity issues have no importance in Christ. Finally, in the obscure term *arsenokoitai*, 1 Corinthians and 1 Timothy condemn abuses associated with homogenital activity in the First Century: exploitation and lust.

So the Bible takes no direct stand on the morality of homogenital acts as such nor on the morality of gay and lesbian relationships. Indeed, the Bible's longest treatment of the matter, in Romans, suggests that in themselves homogenital acts have no ethical significance whatsoever. However, understood in their historical context, the teaching of 1 Corinthians and 1 Timothy, makes this clear: abusive forms of male-male sex—and of male-female sex—must be avoided.

While the Bible makes no blanket condemnation of homogenital acts and even less of homosexuality, this does not mean that for lesbians and gay men anything goes. If they rely on the Bible for guidance and inspiration, lesbians and gay men will certainly feel bound by the core moral teachings of the Judeo-Christian tradition: be prayerful, reverence God, respect others, be loving and kind, be forgiving and merciful, be honest and be just. Work for harmony and peace. Stand up for truth. Give of yourself for all that is good, and avoid all that you know to be evil. To do that is to follow God's way. To do that is to love God with your whole heart and soul. To do that is to be a true disciple of Jesus.

Living by the Bible, gay and lesbian people will submit to those severe moral requirements—and those requirements apply also to sex and to intimate relationships.

That is all that can honestly be said about biblical teaching on homosexuality. If people would still seek to know outright if gay or lesbian sex in itself is good or evil, if homogenital acts *per se* are right or wrong, they will have to look somewhere else for an answer. For the fact of the matter is simple enough. The Bible never addresses that question. More than that, the Bible seems deliberately unconcerned about it.

Sources

Bailey, D. Sherwin (1955). *Homosexuality and the Western Christian Tradition.* London: Longmans, Green & Co.

A comprehensive study of the Bible texts on homosexuality, on which all further contemporary studies rely, though scholars often disagree with Bailey's conclusions. Bailey made the important, though exaggerated, argument that the sin of Sodom was inhospitality and did not involve homosexual intent.

Horner, Tom (1978). *Jonathan Loved David: Homosexuality in Biblical Times.* Philadelphia: Westminster Press.

Another comprehensive and rich study of the Bible texts on homosexuality. Horner impressively focuses on subtle and numerous allusions throughout the Bible that suggest the pervasiveness of homosexual practices in ancient mid-Eastern, including Israelite, societies. Horner suggests a highly probable homosexual relationship between Jonathan and David and a possible one between Naomi and Ruth, and also cautiously alludes to homosexual characteristics in Paul and sensitivities in Jesus.

111

Furnish, Victor Paul (1979). "Homosexuality." In *The Moral Teaching of Paul.* Nashville: Abingdon Press, pages 52-83.

A brief but thorough study of the Christian Testament texts on homosexuality by a specialist in Pauline ethics. Furnish concludes that Romans, 1 Corinthians and 1 Timothy do condemn homosexuality in the form known during the First Century, typified by exploitation and lust. Furnish cautions, however, that contemporary psychological understanding of sexual orientation transforms the discussion significantly, and Paul's teaching alone cannot answer today's questions about the right or wrong of homosexual behavior.

Boswell, John (1980). *Christianity, Social Tolerance and Homosexuality: Gay People in Western Europe from the Beginning of the Christian Era to the Fourteenth Century.* Chicago: University of Chicago Press.

A ground-breaking study of homosexuality from the classic era up to the high middle ages. Boswell argues that Christianity was basically indifferent to homosexuality until the late Twelfth Century and that biblical teaching was not the source of later anti-homosexual Christian attitudes. This book includes a study of all the relevant biblical passages and a long appendix on *malakos* and *arsenokoitai.* On the basis of detailed word studies, Boswell argues that nowhere does the Bible condemn homosexuality *per se.* With strict attention to Pauline usage, Boswell understands *para physin* to mean "beyond the ordinary" rather than the accepted "contrary to nature." The obscure *arsenokoitai,* he insists, refers to a form of male prostitution, not to homosexuality.

Scroggs, Robin (1983). *Homosexuality in the New Testament: Contextual Background for Contemporary Debate.* Philadelphia: Fortress Press.

A thorough and careful study of the Bible and a very useful summary of the classical mindset on homosexuality. Perhaps oversimplifying, Scroggs concludes that the standard "model of homosexuality" in antiquity was pederastic, the relationship between an older man and a younger boy, and that this is what the New Testament condemned in Romans, 1 Corinthians and 1 Timothy. Accordingly, those condemnations do not refer to what is meant by homosexuality today. Scroggs sees *arsenokoitai* as a literal Greek translation of a rabbinic term derived from Leviticus 18:22 and 20:13, and he offers references to rabbinic literature to support his case.

Wright, David F. (1984). "Homosexuals or Prostitutes: The Meaning of *ARSENOKOITAI* (1 Cor. 6:9, 1 Tim. 1:10)."*Vigiliae Christianae* 38, 125-153.

An erudite and detailed review of *arsenokoitai* in post-biblical literature and in the earliest translations of the Christian Testament. Wright rejects Boswell's translation of *arsenokoitai* as male prostitutes and argues that it refers to "homosexuals." Wright points to the Septuagint translation of Leviticus 18:22 and 20:13 as the source of this peculiar Greek term.

Petersen, William L. (1986). "Can *ARSENOKOITAI* be Translated by 'Homosexuals'? (1 Cor. 6:9, 1 Tim. 1:10)." *Vigiliae Christianae* 40, 187-191.

Agrees with Wright's derivation of *arsenokoitai* but criticizes the translation as "homosexuals" because this term reads the twentieth-century understanding of sexual orientation into a first-century text.

Hays, Richard B. (1986). "Relations Natural and Unnatural: A Response to John Boswell's Exegesis of Romans 1." *The Journal of Religious Ethics* 14, 184-215.

Criticizes Boswell's analysis of *para physin* and argues that it does carry the Stoic sense of "contrary to the laws of nature" and that Paul saw homosexuality as a vivid image of human rejection of God's sovereignty and of the order of creation established in Genesis.

Countryman, L. William (1988). *Dirt, Greed and Sex: Sexual Ethics in the New Testament and their Implications for Today.* Philadelphia: Fortress Press.

A study of all the passages on sex in the Christian Testament. Countryman argues that biblical sexual ethics rested on two key concerns: ownership of property (greed) and purity issues (dirt). Understanding Paul's treatment of homosexual acts in Romans as a purity issue, insignificant in Christ, Countryman offers a new and important interpretation obvious in the rhetorical structure of Romans. Thus, he makes further sense of Boswell's study of the Pauline vocabulary in Romans 1. Countryman's discussion of purity issues also provides a broad context for understanding the term "abomination" and its implications in ancient Hebrew society.

Boughton, Lynne C. (1992). "Biblical Texts and Homosexuality: A Response to John Boswell." *Irish Theological Quarterly* 58, 141-153.

A broadly sweeping discussion of biblical texts on homosexuality in light of Boswell's book, though without any attention to Boswell's word study in Romans or mention of Countryman's important contribution on purity issues. Boughton unconvincingly challenges the adequacy of Boswell's argument by suggesting anachronistically that *toevah* refers to something inherently wrong, something contradicting the "fundamental nature" of a thing. Most importantly, Boughton claims that *bdelygma* was not used consistently as a translation of *toevah* to mean things only ritually forbidden. Boughton provides no specific examples or discussion on this critical point. Overall, Boughton merely shows that historical ambiguities surround this discussion.

Biblical Citations

Index

Daniel A. Helminiak, Ph.D.

Daniel A. Helminiak is a pastoral counselor in private practice in Austin, Texas and a Fellow of the American Association of Pastoral Counselors. He completed his Ph.D. in systematic theology at Boston College and Andover Newton Theological School (1979) and an M.A. in psychology at Boston University (1983). At present he is a doctoral candidate (A.B.D.) in educational psychology at the University of Texas at Austin. His research area is adult development.

From 1981 to 1985 he was Associate Professor for Systematic Theology and Spirituality at Oblate School of Theology, San Antonio, Texas. His earlier books are *The Same Jesus: A Contemporary Christology* and *Spiritual Development: An Interdisciplinary Study* both from Loyola University Press. His articles have appeared in publications including *The Journal of Psychology and Theology*, *Spirituality Today*, *Spiritual Life*, *Human Development Anglican Theological Review*, *Pastoral Psychology*, *The Heythrop Journal* and *The Journal for the Theory of of Social Behavior*

Dr. Helminiak was ordained a priest of the Roman Catholic Church in 1967 and is incardinated in the Diocese of Pittsburgh, Pennsylvania.

If you enjoyed this book, consider reading the other important books from Alamo Square Press, dealing with homosexuality and spirituality. You may even wish to send copies of this book and the others to family members and friends.

To order books, send a check for the total cost of books desired plus a postage and handling charge of $2.00 for the first book and 50¢ for each additional book to:

ALAMO SQUARE PRESS
P. O. Box 14543
San Francisco, CA 94114

The publisher will gladly cover sales tax, when applicable.

"When I see the love, caring and forgiveness, joyous living and community among my gay friends and parishioners, I sense the presence of God. When I see the caring and generosity of gay men and lesbians towards those afflicted with AIDS, I see the compassion of Christ. When I see the emergence of gay and lesbian people who claim their dignity, freedom, power and fullness of life, I witness a foretaste of the Kingdom."

In God's Image

Christian Witness to the Need for Gay/Lesbian Equality in the Eyes of the Church

by Robert Warren Cromey
Rector, Trinity Episcopal Church, San Francisco

"There is no false romanticism in the book, rather a keen understanding of the sin and brokenness in which we all share and the forgiving grace by which we obtain health and salvation—all based on an honest approach to the Bible."

— Bishop George West Barrett (from the Foreword)

ISBN: 0-9624751-2-2
128 pages/paperback

$9.95

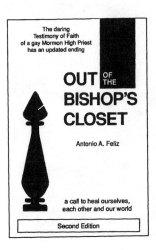

The daring
Testimony of Faith
of a gay Mormon High Priest
has an updated ending

OUT OF THE
BISHOP'S
CLOSET

Antonio A. Feliz

a call to heal ourselves,
each other and our world

Second Edition

OUT OF THE BISHOP'S CLOSET

by Antonio Felix

Tony Feliz knew from childhood that he was drawn to members of his own sex, but as a dutiful Mormon he was convinced by the Elders to marry and raise a family. Tony's faith and hard work brought him up through the ranks of the Mormon priesthood, but the murmurings of his forbidden desires did not leave. With access to the L.D.S. archives, Tony was able to locate the source of Mormon prejudice against gays. He discovered it didn't start with Joseph Smith, who had actually sealed (married) male-male couples, but traced back to Brigham Young and the Victorian Era when the Mormons were forced to desert polygamy.

This book is Tony's story. It reveals not only his anguish, but his ability to forgive a very mortal patriarchy blinded by unlimited power that has lost sight of their human fallibility.

"A bearer of theological promise and spiritual hope to lesbians and gay men who have wrongly suffered rejection and betrayal in the name of God."

Malcolm Boyd, *The Advocate*

ISBN: 0-9624751-7-3
208 pages/paperback

$12.95

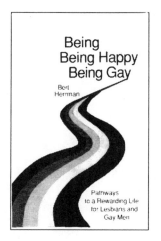

Being • Being Happy • Being Gay

Pathways to a Rewarding Life for Lesbians and Gay Men

by Bert Herrman

"His observations are as clear and lucid as his prose, his message simple but direct: This is a time to not only survive but to thrive. Being gay is a gift, and certainly an ever unfolding mystery. Herrman extends a compassionate and useful hand in the journey toward realizing our full human potential."

— Mark Thompson, Senior Editor, *The Advocate*

"Simple, direct and powerful."

— Julian Baird, *S.F. Sentinel*

ISBN: 0-9624751-0-6
128 pages/paperback

$8.00